Say It With Pictures

Communicators is an imprint of How To Books.
For further details please send for a free copy of the latest catalogue
3 Newtec Place, Magdalen Road, Oxford OX4 1RE United Kingdom

Say It With Pictures

Dr Harry Alder

communicators

Published by How To Books Ltd,
3 Newtec Place, Magdalen Road,
Oxford OX4 1RE. United Kingdom.
Tel: (01865) 793806. Fax: (01865) 248780
email: info@howtobooks.co.uk
http://www.howtobooks.co.uk

First edition 2001

British Library Cataloguing in Publication Data.
A catalogue record for this book is available from the British Library.

Edited by Diana Brueton
Cover design by Baseline Arts Ltd, Oxford

Produced for How To Books by Deer Park Productions
Typeset by Baseline Arts Ltd, Oxford
Printed and bound in Great Britain by Bell & Bain Ltd., Glasgow

NOTE: The material contained in this book is set out in good faith for general
guidance and no liability can be accepted for loss or expense incurred as a result
of relying in particular circumstances on statements made in this book. Laws
and regulations are complex and liable to change, and readers should check the
current position with the relevant authorities before making personal
arrangements.

Communicators is an imprint of How To Books.

Contents

1 Introduction   7

Understand the benefits of simple picture power. Access a world of non-words you never imagined existed.

2 Getting Into Shape   27

The role of lines, shapes and simple graphics that we meet every day, and can all use for better communication, creativity and achievement.

3 Getting Organised   46

Covers everything from rearranging your tiles to organising a wedding, or just doing more with your valuable time.

4 Getting Good Ideas   64

Creativity is an important feature of the human brain, and non-word symbols and shapes have a special part to play.

5 Solving Problems   85

Introduces a few well-known problem-solving techniques that incorporate some graphical element.

6 Giving a Speech or Presentation   103

Most people need all the help they can get in this area. Use more of your natural visual and graphical abilities to do a better overall job of communication.

7 Remembering Things   124

Make the most of your memory by understanding the role of graphical ideas and techniques.

Chapter 1

Introduction

In this chapter:

♦ **Understand the benefits of simple picture power. Access a world of non-words you never imagined existed.**

'I can't draw a straight line.' 'I'm hopeless at drawing.' These are common enough self-beliefs, which are remarkably self-fulfilling and limiting. One wonders why, as an advanced civilisation, we have not ganged together to put such disempowering statements in their place. Instead, amazingly, acting on such irrational self-beliefs, the average well-educated adult can draw no better than a 10 year old.

drawing of woman

by 10 year old

by 43 year old

It's a common ability blind spot, even among the best educated people who, strangely, are not ashamed to admit it. It is culturally acceptable. Thankfully, 'I'm good at drawing', a less common self-belief, has the same self-fulfilling power with the bonus of positive, unexpectedly beneficial consequences.

Whether positive or negative, it seems we establish these sorts of self-beliefs early in life. For instance, careless, deprecating remarks on the part of well-meaning family and teachers can do a lot of damage in later years: 'I've never seen an elephant like that before'; 'that's not a proper circle', and such like.

dog

line

Most of us can recall equivalent self-belief killers in early life and know only too well their long-term influence. It doesn't take much to shatter the hopes of a sensitive young dancer, sportsperson or artist. Conversely, however, little da Vincis with encouraging parents, teachers or mentors go on to a lifetime of pleasure in drawing, art and the worlds they open up. In this case a natural though unspectacular talent may become a pleasurable, therapeutic fulfilling hobby, if not a satisfying career. Just as important, there are spin-off benefits of simple picture power that can affect many aspects of our lives. This book will ensure that you don't miss out on these benefits, however you presently see yourself as a drawer.

A non-drawer is not at all like a non-reader, a non-driver, or a non-listener. Graphophobia fits into the 'I'm tone deaf' and 'I couldn't give a speech if you paid me' categories, which are also high up in the negative self-belief rankings. Like many such beliefs, usually irrational, 'I can't draw a straight line' seems to have attained popular social currency. Strangely, most people are more than ready to reconfirm their limitation, by restating it – usually in a joking way – throughout adult life. Each time they do, they strengthen their negative picture-making self-belief in a hopelessly descending spiral.

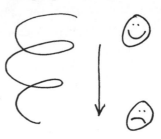

Fortunately, individual competence blind spots don't necessarily mean an overall negative self-image. A low self-image in say, sport or art, doesn't mean 'I'm a complete loser'. A graphophobic may well have a more positive self-image in other areas such as mental arithmetic, word games, gardening, cracking knuckles or getting on with people. There are plenty examples of *empowering* self-beliefs.

These self-beliefs mainly operate unconsciously, which is the way that mental and physical habits are supposed to. There are downsides to negative, habit-based beliefs. We don't realise the extent to which negative self-beliefs are:

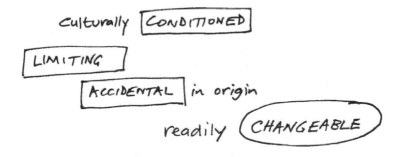

culturally CONDITIONED

LIMITING

ACCIDENTAL in origin

readily CHANGEABLE

Positive self-beliefs, and 'habitual competencies' – doing things without thinking – have quietly ensured our survival and contributed to all manner of unrecognised successes. Ancient cave records confirm the fundamental importance of pictures in this human process.

cave drawing

modern life
drawing

Late developers

Some of us blossom late in our aptitudes and talents. Many people, for instance, take up new hobbies and interests in later years and on into retirement. But there is statistically little chance of late blossoming in basic draughtsmanship other than with a figurative whack on the side of the head. Once established and confirmed by self-fulfilling practice ('I told you I was rubbish'), mindsets of the 'can't' type, however irrational, are of hardier stuff. You have to make the change and acquire the experience and know-how of which the years of negative self-belief have robbed you.

That is not to say that with more positive, childhood nurture today's non-drawers would all have turned out to be great artists. But nor would many 'natural' drawers either. As with any human skill, few reach the very top.

And as well as more or less giving their lives to it, outstanding artists, musicians and sportspeople may well boast a few useful genes that helped them along. Natural drawers are simply more confident in their drawing skills. They are 'unconsciously competent'. They typically apply their natural drawing skills in secondary contexts, such as a hobby or interest, or perhaps a particular aspect of their main work. Most of all, they enjoy simple visual and graphical skills that many others fear or find embarrassing.

What gives pleasure to one person brings pain to another, whether in art, sport, music or whatever.

In the mind

But this is not all down to genetics. Beliefs are all *in the mind*. Thankfully, changing your mind is easier than changing the world around, including other people's minds. That means you can *control* the self-beliefs that play such a big part in your behaviour, achievement and non-achievement. You can *choose* the aptitudes – like simple drawing skill – you would like to foster and perfect. Nothing and no one can stop you.

We tend to enjoy whatever we do well, including doodling or more serious drawing. And the better we get the more we enjoy it. Conversely, we don't enjoy what we believe we are no good at. So we don't do it. So we get even worse. Even the most talented people need to practise their skills. Whatever the origin of a negative self-belief, this process explains how all-pervading it will eventually become in a person's life.

The good news is that what starts in the mind can be changed in the mind. In other words, by changing your mind.

Changing your mind

Just do it

Another important principle is that we sometimes need to *do* something before we enjoy it. In other words – and this applies to any limiting self-belief – you have to abandon inhibition and have a go. This applies to all sorts of things, from trying new kinds of food to a new hobby, interest or holiday destination. Drawing is an ideal starting point, for anybody at any age, as it is typical of the sort of talent of which many people feel they have been short-changed. From a painless start in simple drawing you can build up your confidence in many other areas of your life. This makes the power of little pictures far greater than you might have imagined.

It's important not to feel intimidated or resentful of other people's apparently effortless skills. Not many great contemporary artists can draw a straight line any way. Nor does it matter. Many crafts, and more surreal painting especially, don't involve drawing skills. You can use a ruler to draw a straight line, if it really has to be straight. And a coin or a saucer to draw an impressive circle. If need be, you can find a way to do such things, using a computer. The secret is to *utilise resources you thought you didn't have to achieve things you thought you could never achieve.*

Drawing is another form of self-expression. It helps you to communicate. But it's as much an attitude of mind as a manual skill. Most important, you can enjoy the process as well as the benefits of achievement.

This book is not about 'arty' art – landscapes, portraits, still life, tone, perspective. Nor about modern art, most of which does not remotely call upon draughtsmanship. Nor do I address *drawing* in the freehand, 'natural talent' sense, such as in portrait or still life drawing. You can get that from a night school course or art college, or a book such as *How to Draw Portraits*, or *How to Draw Animals. This book is about getting to know, use and love lines, boxes, circles, squiggles, doodles, shapes – in short, little pictures.* It's about gaining pleasure and having confidence in all sorts of *symbolism beyond words.* It's about believing you *can* draw a straight line *if you need to and when you choose to.* It's about making the best use

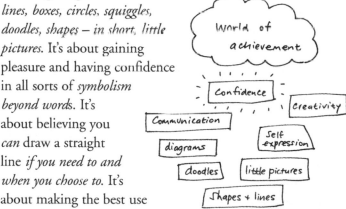

of talents you already have – talents we all have – however latent or atrophied. Having said that, with such confidence, the world of visual arts will soon be open to you. And far bigger worlds of achievement will be within your reach.

Doodlers undaunted

A lot of people are already inveterate drawers without realising it. They make pictures and shapes in order to concentrate, understand, illustrate, communicate, be creative, simplify, persuade, or remember. These people may be described as natural scribblers, born doodlers, embellishers of every variety. They hardly make a phone call without leaving some doodle on the pad. These unsung graphists draw mind pictures. If paper and pencil are not to hand they will unknowingly depict pictures with their fingers, hands, arms and head in three-dimensional space in an attempt to express the pictures inside. They are comfortable with diagrams, figures and illustrations. Some are not too happy with words or numbers. They will use arrows to direct you, asterisks to remind you and all manner of graphical devices to persuade you. And they do it all 'without thinking'. All this is fundamental to the ancient art of doodling. It offers plenty of clues for the would-be picture maker.

If this fits you to some degree, you can celebrate your intuitive skills and develop them to dizzy new heights of pleasure and skill. If you envy such people and want to share their inclination, this is just the book for you. Just to be sure, I assume initial drawing skills of about a 4-

Drawing parallels

What is so special about drawing and pictures as opposed to words and language? First, we could talk about the two sides of your brain. The left side seems to like words, language and other symbols like numbers, and all the logical, sequential thinking that goes with them. The right side works holistically, and reveals an awesome private world of imagery, colours, shapes, ideas and feelings that language cannot cope with. That's the side that is so under-utilised in western culture, especially in our educational and government institutions. In computer terminology, each hemisphere acts like a different operating system. Staying with the analogy, the hemispheres work *in parallel*. Properly used *together* your dual brains can rise to just about any level of human achievement.

Then we could talk about 'sensory preference'. Some people 'think' mainly in pictures, others in sounds and words, while others need to touch, feel and 'experience'. Visualisers are more at home reading a book than listening to an audiotape. They respond to pictures, diagrams or anything visual. The visual sense, besides being the dominant thinking 'modality', is by far the most important sense for everyday communicating. In everyday communicating, you won't get far without it.

Visualising is also strongly associated with inventions and historic, scientific breakthroughs, artistic virtuosity and extraordinary feats of memory. But even everyday skills like spelling depend on visual ability. When matched by equivalent logical, left-brain skills, right-brain imagery starts to take on the characteristics of *genius*. In this sense genius, although rare, is no more than using both sides of your brain and all five senses to their potential. Most of us don't do that because we lost the habit as little children. Orthodox education is left-brain biased. Visual skills, such as drawing, help to redress this imbalance so that we can gain more mileage from a 3lb, bicameral (two-part) brain.

We use our three main senses and both sides of the brain all the time. The trick is to use your brain and your senses *better*. Anyone can do that, whatever his or her brain dominance, sensory preference or however he or she was labelled in the past. Changing the way you think is feasible. It makes sense. At worst it means *changing your mind* – not easy, but possible. The benefits I listed earlier make it very worthwhile.

Disgustingly simple

At one extreme the kind of drawing I will cover in this book is disgustingly simple. Here's a taste. Look at the random words from a dictionary on the next page.

You will remember the circled word. Try as hard as you like, you cannot *not* think about the word with a circle *drawn* round it. The non-word symbol makes the word

Earl	deaf	electrophone	gnash
humble	ignoble	lattice	madam
meteor	monetary	nail	nosing
oracle	outspread	(paddock)	pink
porpoise	prior	quarto	restive
sanicle	submit	three	veloute

special, meaningful and memorable. You register it in a second or less, before you can even begin to digest the other words. That's the power of simple graphics – in this case a roughly drawn circle or oval shape. It's a quick, cheap and most effective way to communicate – in this case one word you want to bring attention to.

There is nothing special about circling a word. I could just as easily have underlined it three times, put a box round it or an asterisk next to it, or used a coloured highlighter pen. The point is that the circle *adds* something. Importantly, it adds more than extra words such as 'notice especially', 'which is very important', etc. In fact, a whole paragraph explaining the significance of one of the words would not have the impact on memory that the simplest non-word would have.

At the same time the non-word, because it sticks out, *detracts* your attention from the other words. But that is fine in this case. First, you probably wouldn't have remembered the other words in any case (we can't handle more than half a dozen things at once), so nothing is lost. Second, it was the writer's *intention* to attract the reader to what he or she considered important. The little circle served a *purpose*. And that's the communication bottom line: a communication is only effective to the extent that it gets what it intended. This may be to inform, warn, persuade, motivate or whatever. In this case the intention was to bring the reader's attention to a particular word, from which to produce some effect in the mind of the reader.

This was accomplished with just an apology for a circle. By adding a whole new graphical armoury to your language you can achieve what you want much more effectively.

A simple picture does something in the brain that a word on its own cannot, or doesn't seem to do well. Having said that, different graphic symbols have a different impact in different situations, and with different people. One symbol, number or shape – just like a word – may be more effective than another. More effective, that is, in helping you achieve your communication outcome. The skill is in understanding when and how to use the rich variety of lines, shapes and symbols at your disposal. If you are already a doodler, what you learn here will add a little science to your intuitive art. Most important, you will gain *practical* know-how in both formal and informal communication, and you will have *practical* ways to generate ideas and solve problems.

More formal examples of pictorial extras might include flowcharts, network diagrams, matrices, graphs, pie charts and such like, most of which are familiar even though you may not use them all yourself. Even the simplest examples can reveal or clarify all sorts of inter-relationships, characteristics and functions that might require volumes of unwieldy prose. However complex the ideas you need to get across, a few simple, graphical 'extras' can make communication simpler and better, and replace thousands of words.

It pays to get to know the power of simple pictures. Everyone can use and benefit from them. They seem more natural to some people, but that comes more from using them habitually (especially if part of your job or hobby) rather than inheriting special genes. The secret is to be *at home* – confident, conversant, and familiar – with non-verbal written communication of any kind. That way you will be able to better understand communications of the sort that appear all the time in newspapers, books and magazines, or reports at work. At the same time you can use graphical techniques such as mind maps to record and recall a meeting or seminar. Or you can use them as part of any communication, whether informally explaining a point to a colleague or in a formal presentation as visual aids.

The techniques you will meet will help you to use your brain to the full, and to get your message across to other people's brains.

Once you accept the principles and acquire the know-how it doesn't require any conscious effort on your part. You just need to harness your natural brainpower, applying the ideas and techniques you learn.

Creativity and better communication are not the only benefits. I will show you how you can enjoy the wide range of benefits I listed earlier, from solving problems and improving your memory to organising your time better. For many, this will uncover a whole world of understanding and expression that translates into day-to-day benefits.

Chapter 2 describes the roles of lines, shapes and simple graphics that we meet every day and can all use for better communication, creativity and achievement. The brain relates to both words and pictures for understanding, remembering, motivating and so on, and this chapter highlights the visual, spatial, 'right-brain' side of things. You will meet the sorts of forms and shapes we meet all the time in graphs, diagrams, hierarchies, flowcharts, matrices and illustrations of all kinds. These turn up everywhere, such as in newspapers, magazines, instruction manuals and on the television. This will give you an idea of the large repertoire of simple visual devices you can use. You will have met these before. But you probably have not used them to the full in different contexts of your life, in new, original ways and to maximum benefit.

Chapter 3 is about getting organised, which covers anything from rearranging your files to locate them easily, to organising a wedding or doing more with your limited time. Chapter 4 is about getting ideas. Creativity is an important feature of the human brain, and non-word symbols and shapes have a special part to play. Chapter 5 illustrates a few well-known problem-solving techniques that incorporate some graphical element. With the right mental approach and some technical know-how you can solve even the most intractable personal problems as if by magic. It's a matter of stimulating your brain to do its job through the sorts of spatial and graphical techniques you have already met. In Chapter 6 we address one of the most common blind spots, even of top managers and many otherwise 'successful' people: giving a speech or public presentation. Most people need all the help they can get in this area. You need never be lost for words if you don't depend on them. Specifically, you can use more of your natural visual and graphical abilities to do a better overall job of communication. Chapter 7 covers memory, and how you can make the best of yours by understanding the role of graphical ideas and techniques.

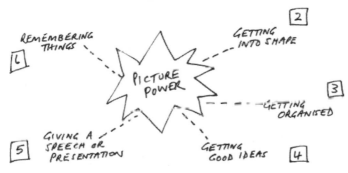

Do it yourself

It's all DIY, so you don't need more books or to attend seminars. Moreover, you can try out what you learn immediately. Thereafter, the more you use the skills, the better you will get. You will soon start to apply what you learn to more important, critical parts of your work and life and clock up real benefits. Our lives are mostly run by habits – useful ones and not-so-useful ones. You will acquire the simple skills I describe as habits by *doing* rather than just *knowing*. That means doing again and again, rather than knowing more and more. Pictures and imagery are a natural and vital part of how we all think, understand and learn. Best of all, you will find a lot of pleasure in extending your mental and manual skills.

I have tried to cater for everybody across the 'drawing a straight line' spectrum. Seasoned drawers or doodlers will, I hope, pick up some useful tips, extend their skills and, especially, make greater use of them. Others may think it is all a bit too simple, strange or stupid and I have tried to anticipate your doubts.

I frequently meet people who initially had no time for a certain sport or pastime, poetry, a particular town or country, an author, artist, entertainer, book, religion or person. Today they are the biggest advocates of what they once rejected or ignored – what was once foreign to their 'map' of the world. That's what comes of giving things a try. It is the way learning should be, as in the process all our maps get richer. The visual representation techniques you will meet in the coming chapters will help you to understand other people's mental maps, enrich your own, and build a rugged bridge between. Just have an open mind, sharpen your mental HB and give it a try.

Here's to :-), world class doodling!

Chapter 2

Getting Into Shape

In this chapter:

◆ **The role of lines, shapes and simple graphics that we meet every day, and can all use for better communication, creativity and achievement.**

A few common geometric shapes, with some simple variations, account for most of the pictures you will meet or ever need for communication and other day-to-day purposes. We use them all the time in diagrams, statistics, flowcharts and suchlike, as well as doodles. They are also indispensable when you need to describe things that are hard to put into words, such as directions to get to a wedding or a customer's factory. We meet these popular lines and shapes in newspapers, magazines, on the television, in books, reports, instruction manuals, road signs and a hundred other instances.

Four-sided shapes

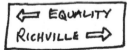

Four-sided shapes are probably the most popular, especially regular ones like squares and rectangles. This is an actual road sign in Fairhope, Alabama.

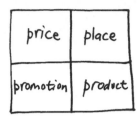

What further mileage can we get from squares, and their close cousins, rectangles?

Chop a square in two and you make four.

Quadrants are a particularly popular variant of squares. You find them in management and training models and textbooks of all kinds. These often display four factors, criteria or issues in a neat, understandable way. You need

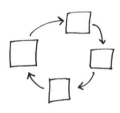

to have exactly four 'things', of course, but hundreds of such models do. Sometimes they illustrate the fact that one quartile relates to the next in a certain direction, then on to the next and so on round.

Matrices are groups of square pigeonholes and extend the scope of the square a lot further. Crossword puzzles are a good example.

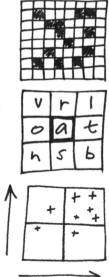

Other popular word games and puzzles like Scrabble and 'make as many words as you can' are also based on squares.

In some cases the upright and horizontal lines of the square form measurement scales, and each quadrant represents the result of one scale against the other. There are many variations on this two-dimensional square model.

Rectangles increase even further the popularity of quadrilaterals. For example, both squares and rectangles appear in profusion in larger diagrams such as flowcharts and hierarchies such as employee organisation charts. In fact four-sided, right-angled shapes turn up in just about any kind of diagram or illustration. Sometimes the shape and size are dictated by the words you need to squeeze inside the shape. Right-angled shapes, like pages in a book, are amenable to enclosing words. Smaller quadrilaterals are fine for one or two words or a heading.

Longer, thinner rectangles feature in bar charts, one of the most common statistical pictures, as well as in time-flow diagrams such as are used for project scheduling.

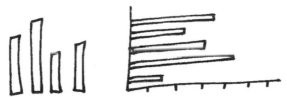

3-D adds to the visual impact of squares and rectangles, and indeed to pictures generally. That's the way things appear in real life. Once you get the idea of drawing a cube, converting these simple shapes to 3-D is a cinch.

Lines without ends

Circles are lines that don't have an end, and come close in the picture popularity stakes. They can substitute for squares in many situations, although you can't write as many words inside them. Circular books, company reports and house deeds are few and far between. Circles also have their curvy cousins, such as ovals, egg shapes and paraboloids.

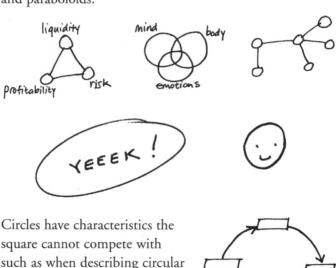

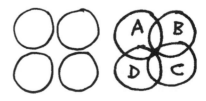

Circles have characteristics the square cannot compete with such as when describing circular type activities and processes that, like a circle, don't end – they just go round and round.

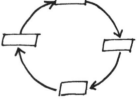

They can also compete with quadrants, but with a struggle, so you don't see many of these.

Circles really come into their own when quartiles don't tell the full story. This applies especially when showing the make up, in fractions or percentages, of a total figure, or any split of a whole into constituent parts. This is sometimes called a pie chart for obvious reasons.

Like bars in bar charts, pie charts can be shown side by side, for instance to illustrate changes over periods of say months or years, or comparisons between different things such as divisions of a company.

JAN   FEB   MAR

Notice the lines I used to crosshatch part of each pie. Lines form the sides of squares and rectangles, as well as circles, but they can do lots of other jobs. Crosshatching is useful, especially when you are working in black and white.

However, the pie chart doesn't do some jobs as well as bar charts.

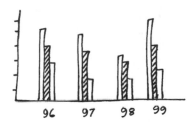

The length of each rectangle can be easily related to a scale at the side, or indeed to an imaginary scale, showing even small changes not apparent from a row of pies.

In fact bar charts can also show
how a total is made up (how the
cake is shared) but not quite as
prettily as pies. Pies and bars are a
matter of taste.

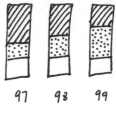

Notice the dots I used to depict a different component of
the bar chart. Dots play a humble but important part in the
scheme of little pictures and I have rarely found
graphophobia extending to this level. Even joining dots into
real pictures comes easily to most people. If you are
confident at doing dots, leave well alone. However, don't be
complacent. Bear in mind that you can create bullet effects
with big dots using a marker pen. And we have already
addressed the utility of dotted lines (mostly little lines rather
than dots) that can denote, for example, indirect
relationships in diagrams such as organisation charts.

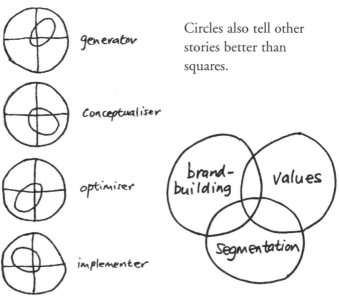

Circles also tell other
stories better than
squares.

In this case the overlapping circles clearly illustrate the interdependent kind of relationship between the parts – usually two or three (try half a dozen and you will see why).

Circles form nodules and other smaller roles in bigger diagrams, just as with squares and rectangles. So in most cases you can take your pick, except that squares are better if you need to incorporate more than a couple of words inside them.

Circles are also used traditionally in certain flowchart type pictures such as critical path networks. In this particular case the circle has its own special meaning, as do the lines and other shapes. The lines represent tasks or individual jobs and the circles represent events – in effect finished tasks, or milestones in a bigger project. This is a case where the meaning of the shape is by some convention or other, so it just comes into its own when you know the convention – i.e. what a circle or square denotes. Otherwise a legend or other explanation makes it clear.

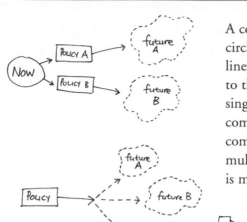

A combination of circles, squares and lines adds significantly to the information a single shape can communicate. Good communication is multi-shape just as it is multi-sensory.

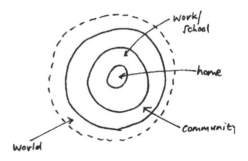

Concentric circles can convey a particular kind of meaning, and some powerful models use this format. In these cases the meanings are fairly obvious.

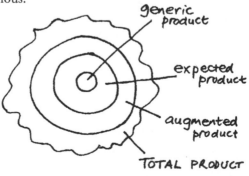

Like very short straight lines used as arrows and dotted lines, parts of circles extend their power almost indefinitely. These appear in the form of sectors, U-shapes, semicircles, curves etc.

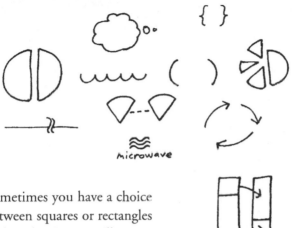

Sometimes you have a choice between squares or rectangles and circles. You can illustrate the popular, so-called 80/20 rule, for example, with either rectangles or circles and sectors.

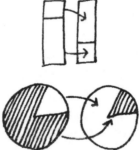

Take your pick, but in this case the rectangles seem to tell the story more simply, just like the side-by-side bars in the

bar chart earlier. However, for a single breakdown of constituent percentage parts – especially if it doesn't need to be too accurate – the shared cake or pie takes some beating.

As we saw earlier, it's when you want to make comparisons over, say, several years, or between different

departments or organisations that bar charts take over.
You can make visual comparisons easily when looking
along them horizontally. Two, or several, percentage
breakdowns can be easily digested in this picture form.

People, as well as all manner of things can be easily
depicted by circles, with a dot or two added.

Amazingly, these simple shapes can also convey feelings
such as pleasure, pain, shock etc.

This illustrates the sort of shorthand our visual sense
uses, such that you can recognise a person, or a person's
disposition, from the scantiest of visual clues. The brain
makes up what is missing from the images and what is
unclear. This, indeed, is the fantastic skill we are
harnessing when using the simplest forms and shapes to
communicate complex ideas. As well as making for an
easier life all round, you can keep both sides of your
brain in better shape to cope with the problems and
opportunities you face.

Lines are even more popular than squares and circles,
which depend on them entirely, whether straight or
curved. Many people don't see a square as just four lines.
Even less do they associate simple lines, whether straight
or curved, with pictures and 'real' drawing. Lines form a

very large part of any professional draughtsman's job. We used lines to produce all the square-type shapes above and curvy lines to produce circles and part circles. The point here is that lines also have a role to play in their own right. Straight lines turn up everywhere and are the basis for most of these graphical techniques.

They are good for denoting connections and relationships.

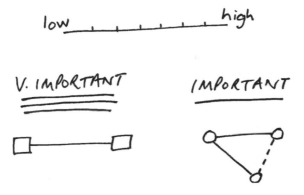

Place a couple of lines at right angles and you have the axes of a graph – another popular line picture that can tell stories with which words would struggle. Graphs can tell lies pretty well, or tell a very convincing but distorted story once you know some of the statistical tricks. Hence they are the graphical stock in trade of economists, political writers and such like.

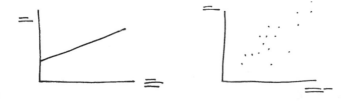

Add a few very short lines
and you have a scale.

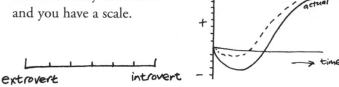

Cross a couple of short lines and you have a cross. You
can use this to place yourself on a scale, for instance, or
to choose from several boxes (squares).

Go crazy on your crosses and
you produce a * or asterisk.
Big ones are good for
highlighting words such as
subheadings on flip charts.

Along with a sword-like asymmetric cross, the asterisk has
found its way into literature of the highest quality. So it's
an example of those very special right-brain little pictures
that compete head on with left-brain words.

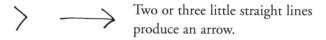

Two or three little straight lines
produce an arrow.

This instantly becomes a
wonder shape that fulfils
many purposes. It can direct
the eye and the mind to
another place quickly and
efficiently. It's a pointer.

The simple arrow forms a vital part of hundreds of diagrams and introduces the whole concept of direction. We would require pages 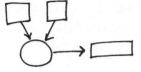 of words and some clever prose to do in words what the arrow picture does for the overworked brain in an instant. In a line type diagram such as a flow-chart, for instance, do you 'think' from top to bottom, left to right, up right toward north east and so on? The arrows help you do it 'without thinking'. When depicting movement, or a process, in which direction (eg clockwise or anticlockwise) does it go? Just point yours arrows.

Arrows can also represent force, as in the popular force field analysis diagram.

In this case positive forces are compared with negative forces, such as in tackling a problem. That is, things that help towards your goal, and things that slow you down or mess things up. Getting these on paper helps to focus the mind on factors you need to reduce or eliminate and those you need to increase because they are helping you towards a solution. Psychologically, transposing little arrows for these sometimes worrying issues depersonalises them. They are just forces, which you can deal with objectively, one at a time. No one is out to get you, and you don't need to feel angry or guilty.

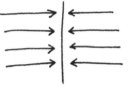

Big or thick arrows can represent big forces and little ones little forces. This introduces weighting, which makes this tool even more useful, as a single factor might be more important than several others and therefore justifies more of your attention.

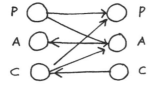 Circles and arrows combined are popular. Transactional analysis, which is concerned with parent–adult–child interrelationships, is a good example of this graphical duo.

Arrows can have a bit of substance and form beyond simple lines and in this way they can easily incorporate large words, or a lot of little ones, when they are needed. They can easily denote meaning in symbols or logos.

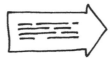

Three lines joined together also make a triangle, of course, so you can't stop these cropping up. You are then into yet another world of pictures. Triangles are great 'off the peg' shapes that combine well with other shapes, and are ideal when you have three points or topics to get across.

A triangle soon becomes a pyramid. As well as being a lovely stable thing, the pyramid boasts a wide base and a narrow top. This arrangement suits many business and other models and diagrams. For example, organisation hierarchies (with one boss and lots of lower rank workers) and other hierarchies such as genealogies. Or systems that build up one step after another.

Turn it upside down and it becomes very unstable. This can illustrate systems that are top heavy. Or it may be used when large numbers, such as customers or production workers, are important, and are shown at the top of the organisation.

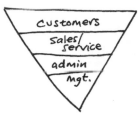

Irregular four-sided shapes are not nearly as popular as squares, rectangles and equilateral triangles. But even these have uses in communication. Measurement enveloping two scales can sometimes be depicted as an irregular, four-sided shape. This is often the case with

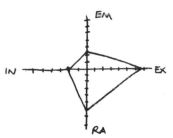

psychometric tests, which represent a person's score, say on a scale between introvert and extrovert on one axis, and between emotive and rational on the other axis.

Curves play an important part. These are sometimes regular like parts of a circle, and sometimes very irregular.

Some curves keep recurring, such as the classical 'normal distribution', or Gaussian (after a M. Gauss) curve. Whenever you spot this shape you know it represents the 'natural' range of frequency – the sort you would get when measuring people's heights or the size of leaves (and a few million other natural phenomena), or, say economic statistics that *involve* people and their random behaviour. Such frequency measurements tend to hover mostly around the average or norm with a few extremes at the high and low end, falling off in a very predictable way.

Similarly this sort of shape, when skewed one way or the other, indicates greater frequencies at one end or the other. You might get this if you measured punctuality at a factory or school for instance. That is, a rapid falloff from the norm not many minutes before starting time with a more gradual frequency falloff as the morning wears on. A skewed curve can represent all sorts of situations. A product or organisation life circle is a common example of such an irregular, but typically skewed curve. Sales and profitability of a particular product, for instance, rise then fall away gradually but separately after they reach a fairly early peak.

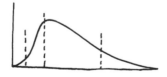 

With special promotion you may be able to boost a product's fortunes and extend its life. This may happen several times and the product curve shows this graphically.

Three- and four-sided shapes are without doubt the most popular. But you can just as easily have shapes with five, six, seven sides and so on. However, it gets a bit harder to draw them without instruments, and that can be a chore. Nevertheless, when you have five points to make, or five main topics to cover, you can't do better than use a pentagon or divide a circle into five segments.

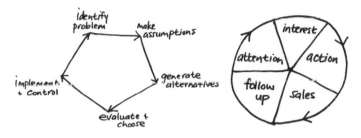

Hexagons are a bit easier to draw. This one is another actual road sign spotted in Shreveport, Louisiana.

You can create a similar sort of diagram using a circle divided into segments, but again, with five you have the same problem of getting your angles reasonably accurate. Otherwise keep to spoke-type lines and a central circle or square. That way it doesn't look so obvious when the overall shape is out of alignment.

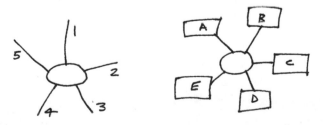

There is no great transition between these simple geometric shapes and simple, 'real' drawings depicting

objects or people. For instance, Maslow's famous 'hierarchy of needs', illustrated often with stacked rectangles like a pyramid, is sometimes termed a ladder. In this case what better than a ladder drawing to illustrate its meaning.

The same idea could be used for any system where one component builds on another or a process 'climbs' to a higher level. Similarly, if you want to illustrate relative importance or weighting, why not use a simple seesaw scales picture? In these sorts of cases your 'real' drawing doesn't need to stray much from the well-known geometric shapes we have already met. The meaning is obvious.

Some shapes, like irregular stars, can grab attention.

We sometimes underestimate how we depend on simple, 'stylised' figures. These are the equivalent of a stenographer's shorthand. It's a fast, reliable way to communicate that transcends language and culture.

The ubiquity of lines and simple shapes means we can't ignore them, and their impact on our lives, for too long. Hopefully their new found familiarity might also reduce the irrational fear that some readers have of putting little pictures to paper when occasion requires. The range of shapes and non-word symbols in this chapter probably covers about 90% per cent of the graphical representations used in everyday 'static' visual communication such as in newspapers, books, magazines, reports and even statistics on television. They also represent the lion's share of graphical techniques used for problem solving, remembering, learning, note-taking, getting organised, generating ideas and opportunities and so on. Most importantly, you can draw every one of them if you decide to, and all the variations your creative mind can concoct. That means you will have extra tools beyond words to help in self-development and achievement generally.

Chapter 3

Getting Organised

In this chapter:

◆ **Everything from rearranging your files to organising a wedding, or just doing more with your valuable time.**

Pictures can help you do more with your time and generally get organised. People who tend to plan what they do achieve more than those who don't. That may well just tell us about people who plan on paper, however, as some people plan things in their mind before dropping off to sleep and don't consider that planning. Nonetheless, simple shapes and pictures can help.

Networks

I'll start with one of the most advanced graphical planning processes, but will show how simple graphics make it powerful. PERT stands for Programme Evaluation Review Technique and it has its origins in the US military. For present purposes that's network planning, or critical path analysis. It has been used for planning and controlling some of the biggest projects in the world, such as underground rail systems, dams and military aircraft development. It helps to plan and control what may be a complex project in such a way that you complete it in the minimum of time, and on budget. In particular that means thinking ahead, so that you do each task or make arrangements early enough to avoid delays at some later stage.

For instance, if you are adding a house extension you don't want to find half-way through you are waiting for some tool or material, or building regulations approval, or that you didn't book a plasterer ahead. A task may just take half an hour but if you don't schedule it properly it may hold you up because it depends on something else being finished – something which could have been planned ahead. Here's a very simple network analysis.

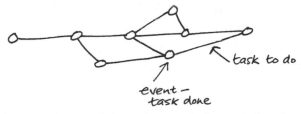

The critical part of the technique is the critical path. That is the sequence of jobs and tasks that will result in the shortest overall project time.

Doing this sort of analysis means you have to do a lot of thinking before you start. As well as identifying every little task in the overall project jigsaw (sometimes the details cause the biggest delays), you need to determine the order in which they come because one thing may depend on something else. In other words, each part of the project is related to every other part. Knowing how critical each relationship is, in terms of timing and cost, will help you to complete the overall project in the minimum time. In the above little network you will see the critical path.

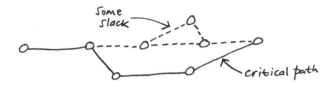

This is an ideal technique if you are getting married. Even a fairly small wedding needs an Einstein to get everything right just in time for the big moment. It is also helpful when moving house or carrying out building work, or whenever you have a non-negotiable deadline. It means you have to, in effect, work backwards from your end date, in order to know the latest date and the earliest date on which you can do, or start to do, a particular individual task. If there is 'slack', that's fine. Slack means you can wait a little while – maybe to save cost or concentrate on other tasks – without jeopardising the final completion date. Every individual task for which there is no slack will lie on the critical path, which is where you need to devote your best brains.

For instance, if you are building a house extension you can order the carpet as soon as you know the room size, which you have to determine very early anyway. That is, if you've got somewhere to store it. Or you arrange to buy the paint as soon as you have chosen your colour scheme. That simply means better planning, but an investment in planning usually pays off. I say usually, because the PERT technique concentrates on planning and control efforts that will affect the final deadline – and ultimate success. This is not planning for planning's sake, which doesn't go down too well with right-brain dominant people anyway.

Similarly, you can't carry out the electrics until the plastering is finished, or start the plastering until certain construction work is done. However, you can get the materials in stock a week or two earlier if it's a DIY job. Or you can make a firm booking for an electrician as soon as you have a good idea of when the plasterer will be finished. If you don't know about these basic tradespeople interdependencies, then one of your leading tasks is to find out. It doesn't require rocket science, just thinking ahead, which is where these graphical techniques help.

There are two certainties about a wedding, house move or any other complex activity. One, you will forget things and make mistakes. Two, these will tend to be in critical areas. That means that your critical path network has to show a dynamic, ever-changing picture. Otherwise it's as good as useless and a task you could have done without. Timings and relationships will inevitably change, and a new critical path appears as soon as you turn your back.

However, all is not lost. By concentrating on just the new critical tasks and timings, you know that every day or hour you save (say by throwing energy and money at the problem) will help towards achieving your final deadline. The trick is to do everything you can as soon as you can. That way, if you do run into problems you can devote all your time and attention to it rather than spending valuable time on jobs that could have been long since put to bed.

These techniques are not magic and they don't mean you can bypass your brain.

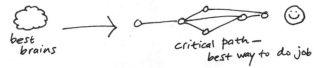

You cannot avoid, for instance, having to identify the many tasks that go to make up a successful project. If you miss a couple of key ones, then no technique will save you. Similarly, unless you can establish the interdependencies – what needs to happen in what order – you may as well spend your time fire-fighting rather than planning.

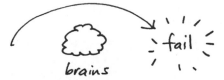

However, the process – especially if it is laid out graphically to make it easy on your brain – helps you see to what you need to do anyway.

Effort vs. results

A universal rule says that we spend most of our time and effort on a minority of the important results we achieve, and much less time on things that are really important and contribute to our long term goals.

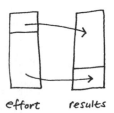

This is called Pareto's Law after the Italian economist who promulgated it, and is best illustrated in a diagram.

This is a good picture to keep in your mind if you want to be well organised. It reminds us that we spend most of our time on things that are not important for achieving our goals, and relatively little time on important things.

A graph tells the same story about human nature. This is the effort-results curve. It tells the same story using a different picture. The principle of creativity means reversing this curve, so that you get maximum results from minimum effort.

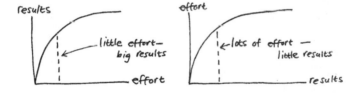

This doesn't mean being lazy – just using your brain in the right way. Another sinister rule says that after you have tried to correct the Pareto phenomenon in your life you will lapse back into the same ubiquitous ratio.

Picture your future

The best way to get organised is to organise your life from time to time. That means deciding on your long-term goals, and how you intend to fulfil them – strategies for success. We usually find that we have a hierarchy of goals, and each short-term goal contributes towards achieving a higher one, which in turn (we hope) contributes to achieving our life goals. The triangle or pyramid is the shape to illustrate this phenomenon. It illustrates the fact that many day-to-day activities support a fairly short list of intermediate goals, which in turn support – or contribute towards – our long-range goals, which in turn fulfil our beliefs and values.

Short-term issues are many; long-term issues are few. The unimportant things in life are many; the important things are few. These represent the precious, thin air at the top of the giant pyramid of your life.

Another way to be well organised is to sort out your values – what is important. Values also form part of a hierarchy, as we tend to direct our behaviour towards them just as with major goals. Goals reflect your values just as values reflect your goals. Although we express them differently, they are two sides of the same coin.

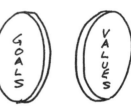

As you realise the interdependence of values and personal goals you can deliberately start to get them in line. *Congruency* in your life is a sure way to achievement and satisfaction.

Pay attention

You need to stay alert and concentrate, especially when things are complicated and you need to get your mind organised. We all have a natural attention span, which is a lot less than many teachers and trainers seem to believe.

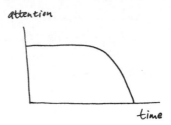

You can make a couple of common-sense conclusions from this.

First, you need to break big jobs down into little parts. This is not just so that you can get your mind round them, but also so that each task fits within your normal concentration span.

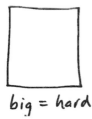

big = hard

little = easy

Second, make sure you don't have interruptions that will ruin your concentration. This just takes a few moments' planning. It may not be worth starting certain jobs if you can't be sure of a reasonable uninterrupted period to yourself.

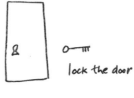

lock the door

Funky files

Pictures and individual symbols (including alphabetic letters on their own or in couples, like AA) register very quickly on the brain, which is why company logos can quickly be identified on a busy high street. This is a useful principle for getting organised, such as filing – the bane of many a creative person's life. I use little pictures, symbols or icons on the spines of most of my files.

If a client or the subject is known by a logo, I use that, simply cutting it out of a letterhead and sticking it onto the spine of the file. It seems a shame not to make use of well-established company logos after so many millions have been poured into them over the years. Depending on your business, you can apply the same principle to suppliers, clients, banks, VAT and so on – wherever there is a well known symbol or logo.

A picture may not paint a thousand words but it will usually save you half a dozen at least. However, if you don't trust your ability outside words, use both. The icon, logo or other little picture will take you quickly to the file you are looking for, and the words will confirm the exact subject matter, such as 'Far East consultancy' or 'VAT returns from 97/98'. If you are a creative doodler/drawer, you will probably enjoy graphical systems anyway. We read enough words over the course of a day anyway so imagery helps to keep the right-brain perky.

The same labelling method can be applied to floppy discs and CD ROMs, the fronts of reports and so on. In short, you can use little pictures for just about any sort of labelling or identification to make organising easier.

Usually a filing system is hierarchical, so how do you accommodate such complexities using naïve little pictures? Main categories of files can be in different coloured files. There is plenty of choice nowadays. Everything doesn't have to be buff or dark grey. Subdivisions can be identified in a similar way, such as by a certain shape or colour sticker to represent a subject area.

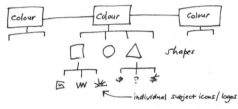

A simple application for a writer/consultant could be three different coloured files to represent UK, Europe and rest of the world – that is, basic geographic or regional divisions. These will be separate physically, of course, which is an obvious visual principle when organising. Next, publishers could have a square sticker (for anywhere in the world, ie on any of the three file colours), titles (books) a white round sticker, administrative type files a blue triangle and so on. Put the sticker in the same place on every file so that your eye immediately identifies its main type. Different coloured and shaped stickers – readily obtainable – extend the degree of classification even further.

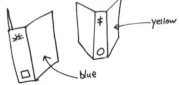

The next level of visual identification is the logo or little picture I started with. In some cases a couple of alphabetical letters are as easily recognisable as a picture.

This depends on the associations the letters have. For instance a book on intelligence I wrote was identified with the letters IQ, and another on emotional intelligence, EQ. Similarly 'e' now has its own significance in the world of the internet, thus forming its own 'picture' of meaning.

Once again, those of a nervous disposition can add a few words in addition to a colour or shape. Using the same example, you can add the full title of a book, or the full name of a company. This keeps your left-brain as well as your right-brain happy. You will probably find that the words are soon redundant anyway, and that unconsciously you are just drawn towards well-known shapes and colours. A more pragmatic reason for words as well as pictures is if a number of people are using the same system. Most people, however, associate with a well-known logo.

Taking notes

You can use graphics in note-taking, such as in a training course, for meeting minutes or a record of any conversation. That doesn't mean you have to launch into icons and pictures. Simply use the wheel and spoke or a hierarchy format as you would when brainstorming. The subject forms the centre of your mind picture. In the case of a recurring meeting it might just be the name of the meeting and date. Each topic covered forms a main spoke and each issue or decision within that topic forms a lower level branch and so on. For minutes or notes taken at a meeting, one branch can be for those attending. You can thus accommodate any aspect of minute-taking in this graphical format, as a complete, reliable draft to be word processed afterwards. If you need a word for word record (less common nowadays) you would be safer tape-recording the whole meeting.

This note-taking application of graphics is particularly helpful in a training situation. It helps you to get a structure to the whole subject, which helps you to understand and remember it. The central place of the subject on your page means that you cannot help coming back to it, to see the 'big picture'. Usually the trainer is competent enough to let you know what his or her main headings are, perhaps as a list of words or phrases at the beginning on a flip chart or OHP. The same will apply to subheadings. Your wheel and spoke skeleton means that you are watching out for this vital information so will not miss it amidst interesting anecdotes and incidental references. By getting this down in a non-linear way you will establish it in your mind within a sensible structure that *you understand*, simply because you recorded it in that way. When you refer back to your mind picture you will not be faced with pages of words and no immediate picture of how all the topics and subtopics relate to each other. As we shall see in Chapter 7, pictures do wonders for your memory.

Usually an A4 sheet of paper will hold an enormous amount of information at a sufficient level of detail to trigger your memory about further detail, anecdotes etc. Confining say a training session of perhaps a couple of hours into a single sheet of paper is also a good mental discipline, as you are required to summarise drastically, and express things in your own words. It may be too ambitious if you are taking notes over days rather than hours. In that case simply start a sheet for each main topic, as if you had chopped off a main branch of your hierarchy tree or a main spoke of a wheel, starting a new wheel.

If you are brave, you can introduce little pictures into this note-taking format. The principle is simple: we remember simple pictures more easily than phrases or sentences, and often more than individual words. Put another exaggerated way, a picture paints a thousand words. The secret is to choose the picture representation yourself, intuitively, just as you choose a couple of words to remind you of a topic. Whatever picture you dream up will have special meaning to you, and will be much more effective than if the trainer him or herself chose a graphical representation.

The picture needs to be appropriate, of course, but not logical in any literal sense. Usually the picture that immediately comes to your mind will be the most appropriate for you – that's why your brain presented it to your conscious mind.

Most people are slow to risk thinking in pictures – at least when it comes to getting their thoughts down on paper. Usually, this is not because nothing visual comes to mind to represent the words we would otherwise have had to use. It's because we don't trust ourselves to remember what we meant by a particular little picture when we revisit our notes. This is one of the main purposes of note-taking, of course, especially if it is a formal record such as of a meeting. That's just a matter of confidence. In practice it is almost impossible not to associate a 'picture equivalent' with the subject that initially triggered the association. Try it. When you use your brain to the full – which means using your inner senses, especially the super powerful visual sense – it's a lot harder to forget than to remember. However, as with anything worthwhile, it takes commitment and a little practice before valuable habits are formed.

Organisation charts

These are one of the most common kinds of pictorial organisation tools that we meet early in our careers. They rarely adopt other than the traditional hierarchy format that crops up everywhere.

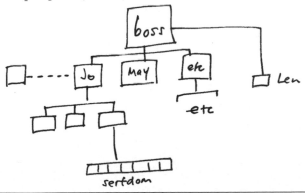

Nonetheless, a simple person hierarchy tells a big story. Who reports to whom? Who is responsible for a function or division of work? How do people in different functions compare in level of seniority (and probably salary) within the organisation? What horizontal or dotted-line relationships exist and so on? You would need a very wordy report to tell this story.

This one shows a functional or departmental organisation rather than people.

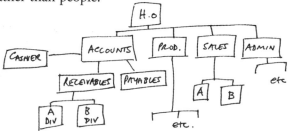

Some organisations add more pictures in the form of photographs of each person. This adds a new dimension to a faceless hierarchy, and it instantly becomes a very different sort of communication tool.

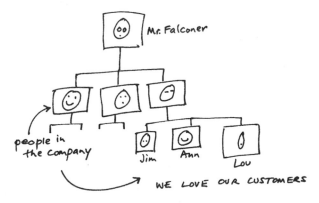

Wall diary systems

Wall chart diary systems are a simple representation of a desk diary system with its many pages. It's all on a single sheet, just like the A4 notes we discussed earlier. Even on a wall rather than brief-case scale, that means that space is limited. You are therefore more likely to have a square inch to play with for each day than anything up to a whole A4 page in a day-a-page diary (which is rarely used anyway by productive people who tend not to be diarists). A square inch is great for visual techniques, as it concentrates the mind and forces you to keep words to an absolute minimum.

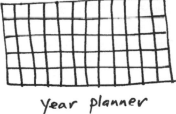

Year planner

Fortunately the Pareto rule says that hardly a fifth of all our wall chart planning accounts for about four-fifths in terms of its importance to our job and life. But implicit in this rule is the fact that a lot of our lives boil down to repetition and routine. Even company chairpeople and prime ministers have recurring tasks. They might not seem like routine from where you and I sit, but at a certain level almost anything can be relegated to a mental back burner, or be carried out on mental autopilot.

In terms of a diary system, you don't have to repeat words for every, say, weekly or monthly meeting, client visit and so on. A blue circle could represent a Monday morning staff meeting, so all you need is blue circles stuck or drawn in each Monday square (at the top left which allows you plenty of room for more little pictures). If you don't associate weekly staff meetings with blue circles – or whatever shape, icon or little picture you care to choose – you soon will, just as you get familiar with road signs or any common symbols. We met the same memory principle when discussing labelling files using colours and simple shapes. Better still if your little picture already has an association. But that is more important in the case of non-recurring events where you do not have the advantage of the automatic memory power of repetition.

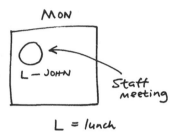

A little creativity will not be wasted when designing a system such as a wall chart diary planner. If your life is full of meetings, a circle (or a large marker pen dot) could represent a meeting; different colours could represent different kinds. A further level of meaning might be a single word, inside the circle or next to the dot. For instance, if green circles represent regular six-monthly staff appraisal interviews you conduct as a manager, the name of the person concerned is all you need to add (and even that can be initials). That tells the

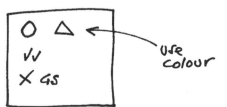

whole story and you will instantly recall what you have to do on a particular day.

Time of day, as well as name, may be another variable. But again, you don't need to write 10am for a regular, 10am Monday meeting. You just need little pictures to remind of what you might forget, not what you couldn't forget (that the weekly staff meeting always starts at 10am or that GS is George Scholes). Here we have a combination of creativity, ingenuity and simple common sense. Given these, there is hardly any limit to the degree to which you can plan your weeks and months and be reminded of whatever is important with hardly a glance.

Chapter 4

Getting Good Ideas

In this chapter:

◆ **How creativity is an important feature of the human brain, and non-word symbols and shapes have a special part to play.**

We think in pictures as well as words. The visual sense is the most important in everyday life and takes up a lot more physical brain space than the other senses. Several aspects of the right-brain are concerned with imagery and this side is particularly linked with creativity. We sometimes call a creative, lateral thinker a 'right-brain thinker'. We have already seen how pictures play a big part in our lives. In this chapter we will see the role that visual methods play in creativity, or getting good ideas. You may learn something new about the process and principles of creativity .

Usually we don't think about thinking. When it comes to creativity it sometimes seems we are not thinking at all. It just happens. Ideas seem to come from nowhere. This mostly happens at an unconscious level, which is a characteristic of the right-brain. Some brain functions can only work when we don't know they're working. As well as any habitual behaviour we do without thinking, these include 'eurekas', flashes of inspiration, insights – all those creative sorts of things.

Fortunately, although we don't know how these things work, we can stimulate creative thoughts in different ways, and particularly by the use of pictures and visual techniques.

What does this word bring to your mind?

SLETAR

What does this picture bring to your mind?

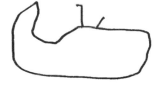

Both the word and the picture are nonsense, having no meaning in themselves. However, most people will manage to make a meaning out of a nonsense picture more easily than out of a nonsense word. The left-brain operates happily in words and other symbols. If it can't come up with an association for a nonsense word, it calls it a day. However, the right-brain draws on the unlimited resources of your memory (comprising billions of sensory experiences) and unconscious mind when interpreting shapes and visual images. It keeps going and doesn't stop until you (using your conscious left-brain) stop it. We see things everywhere – in fire, clouds, wallpaper patterns and ink blots. So if you want to dig deep into your mind for ideas, memories, inspiration and solutions to problems, pictures will help enormously.

Shapes and pictures conjure up meaning. But, having said that, very few words have no meaning if you think about them long enough. The word SLETAR reminded me of a sitar, an Indian musical instrument. Then I thought of a slot. However, I had to use my imagination to do that. You probably thought of something quite different. Imagination is the sights, sounds and feelings inside us. I happened to see and hear a sitar, and I could also see and feel a slot. After a few moments' reflection the word – any word – will no doubt bring new thoughts, or even a string of thoughts, to your mind. As we have already seen, the visual sense is all pervading, so even when we use words and language, pictures play a big part. For instance, it has been found that the best 'natural' spellers always use visual techniques.

$$Cat$$

Remarkably, sound can make for bad spelling, as illustrated by the absurdity of rough (ruff), bough (bow), thought (thort), coughed (coft), eight (ate), light (lite), indict (indite), impugn (impune).

Why be creative?

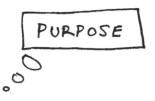

There is little point in being creative unless you need to do something that requires creativity, or have a problem to solve or a difficult goal to reach. In other words creativity, like anything worthwhile, should have a purpose.

It's hard to kid your unconscious mind. It's the honest part, as evidenced particularly in dreams, which don't spare any blushes. So it might not be too cooperative if it thinks it is wasting its time. The stronger your purpose, or the more compelling your goal, the more likely your creative mind will click into gear. For example, if you have to find money by the weekend to keep the bailiffs away, you tend to think of ways to get money you would never otherwise have thought of. Need turns on the creative juices.

Given a decent reason to be creative you don't need to be a 'creative person'. That is a misleading idea anyway. Creativity is a way of thinking, which we all use from time to time, rather than a fixed personality trait. It's true that some people think creatively more than others. That may be because they have learnt how to do it, or their job requires it, or in their case circumstances and even survival demand it.

So instead of 'I want to be creative', why not 'I'd like to find a creative way to . . .'

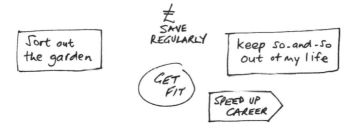

That literally concentrates the creative mind. It focuses your creativity.

'Creative' may mean a:

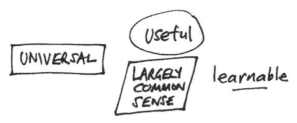

way of doing something or achieving a goal. Seriously lazy people are quite rare and they can teach us a lot about creativity. They often turn out to be quite productive, as well as creative, because they learn to do important things with minimum effort.

In this respect creativity is just part of the way we think, act and live normally. The point is we don't do things for nothing. Every behaviour – including habits we do without thinking – is to bring about some end or other. We precede every action with a thought. Again, this might be a conscious thought ('I'll ring her now to check . . .') or an unconscious thought. This includes things we do instinctively, 'without thinking' (we are not aware of thinking), or as a reaction against some danger. For instance, we don't instinctively duck, blink, freeze or scream except if some outside sound, sight or sensation triggers a possible source of real danger. Similarly (this is my idea anyway) you don't turn on the creative juices unless something in your brain conscripts them. Put another way, we do everything with a purpose 'in mind'.

'Unconscious intention' is a big psychological subject and comprises the many things that motivate us other than

conscious acts of will. But for present purposes let's just say
you have to 'think' (use your brains in some way) to do
anything. The better the ideas or insights, the better – or
more effective – your behaviour and the results you achieve.

Creativity is:

Most of all, creativity is not confined to so-called creative
people, creative professions, or creative activities like
advertising, interior design and product development.
You can use the same creative techniques to think of ideas
for a business venture, new product or room décor as you
can to solve specific problems. The difference is just
semantics. They are all goals or purposes you want to
reach or achieve. In the case of a problem your goal is to
solve it. Better still, to be in the positive state you wish
such that you don't have a problem. That is, you
concentrate on what you want (some new 'state') rather
than what you don't want (the problem, or your present
'state'). In each case
you are at A and you
want to be at B.

Call it what you like, but you need to move – do
something. And that's where creative thinking comes in.
You want to get to where you want to be as easily,
cheaply, pleasurably etc as possible.

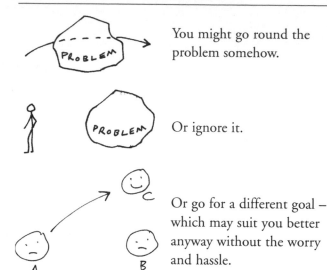

You might go round the problem somehow.

Or ignore it.

Or go for a different goal – which may suit you better anyway without the worry and hassle.

The possibilities of creative thinking (and creative behaviour) are infinite. That's what human creativity means. You can even solve a problem in such a way that you are better off than you would have been even without it. In other words, you turn a problem to your advantage. It becomes an opportunity. This is very useful stuff, but very much underrated and under exploited because of the predominance of left-brain thinking in western culture.

In this chapter you will be reminded of what you probably already knew about how little pictures can help you to think creatively and achieve a lot, more easily and quickly.

This is a sun or a hub of a wheel with spokes coming out.

In fact you can easily think of more than 15 things it is:

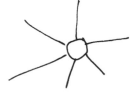

1. An insect with too many legs.
2. etc.

Write your purpose in the middle.

That is the subject you want to have brainwaves, or good ideas, about – your goal. It need not be specific. For instance, you might just want some creative ideas about your:

Or whatever. Write a word or two in the middle to record, inside this little picture, what you want of your creative mind.

Now relax. If you find a certain kind of music helps, put some on.

You are now going to come up with ideas about your purpose – lots of them. If you don't, it doesn't matter, but you will anyway.

As an idea comes to you write it down as one of the spokes coming out of the hub. Do it quickly, as sometimes ideas come so thick and fast that they are gone before you know it. So keep your ideas to one or a few words. Provided you know what you mean, you will be surprised at how easily your mind recalls just what you had in mind from a word or two.

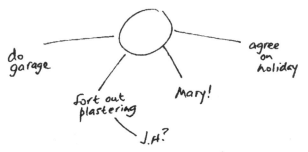

In fact pictures are even better. If you wish, you can use pictures throughout. For instance, for a money issue you could put a pound or dollar sign in the middle (depending on whether you want to rake in pounds or dollars).

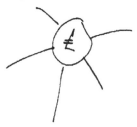

This saves time, spelling, brain wear and tear, etc. It is also the right mode for our visual, creative brain.

Word and language are strongly associated with the left-side of the brain, along with logic such as we use in maths and computer programming. The sight of a mass of words naturally fires the left side of the brain that handles them best. But to get plenty of good ideas you need to be in right-brain, creative mode, so it makes creative sense (whatever the logic) to avoid left-brain symbolism (i.e. words or numbers).

Having said that, often a combination is best. That is, a little picture and a couple of little words.

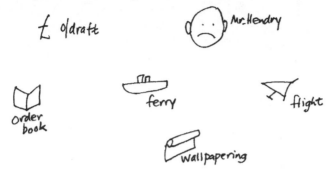

The picture reminds you of the idea, and the words add a bit more detail. As each idea comes, add another spoke.

Sometimes more ideas come once you have gone down a particular spoke. For instance, if one of your spokes on a money issue is borrow, you might then think of bank, children's moneybox, or rich Aunty Nell. Make each new idea a branch of a main spoke.

So now your picture is not so much a wheel but like a tree looking from above. To each branch you can add little branches then twigs. You don't have to, but you have the flexibility so that you will always have somewhere to get your ideas down as they start to flow.

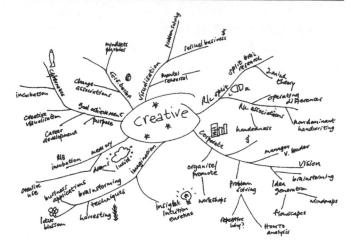

As you get further down a branch the ideas usually become more practicable. If you keep going you will finish with a 'to do' list you can start to carry out immediately.

If you're not into wheels or birds eye views of trees don't despair. A simple hierarchy or tree format will do the same job. What is sometimes called a balloon diagram is one example.

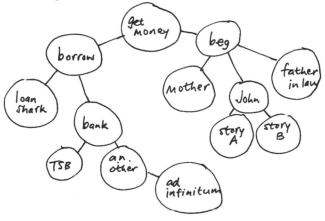

This one uses words, to illustrate how it usually appears, but the principle of working in little pictures applies very widely. The aim is simply to get more creative ideas so whatever works best for you is best for you.

The hierarchy or cascade format of the balloon diagram means that you tend to start with just two or three main branches, each of which expands with a few subsidiary ideas and so on. The advantage of the 360 degrees sun or wheel and spoke format is that you have room for lots of initial ideas stemming from the main purpose. That lends itself to a brainstorming type process in cases where you haven't begun to produce even a basic tree-type hierarchy. On reflection, which is part of the creative process (but not the first stage), you may spot that only two or three of your initial spokes are the main areas to explore, and the rest fall somewhere within those main branches. Second or third time round, a balloon diagram might fit the bill better. This doesn't mean you chop off initial spokes. That can quash ideas that seem stupid but that may turn out to be truly innovative. It just means you can move them around within the structure of your mind picture so that they relate better to the overall creative purpose. Also, by keeping all your initial brainstorm spokes on paper, if you come to a dead end on what you thought was a winner you can always come back to reconsider them.

We write from left to right in our culture and that also influences the way we think, in ideas as well as language. So you could express an earlier branch or hierarchy type picture on its side growing towards the right. Do what

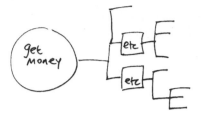

works best for you. In this case 'best' is simply the volume of ideas you can come up with in a short time. In other words, it's about creativity rather than analysis and judgement, which come later and require a different mode of thinking.

This format suggests another important aspect of creative thinking. Sometimes you get a bright idea but can't, or don't relate it to an end purpose. You can see no immediate use for it. But we usually know a good idea when we get one. So the question in this case is what (existing) purpose might this out-of-the-blue idea help towards? Or, how can I make it *useful?*

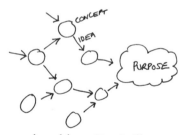

What is known as the Concept Fan does just that.

It is usually used for problem solving, working backwards to arrive at the real problem. But it illustrates the rather profound idea that every idea that ever flashes through our mind will relate, however tortuous the route, to a goal or purpose. That makes us take creativity more seriously. It starts to make sense in day-to-day achievement as well as in a survival sense.

Sometimes creative thinking works in a fairly linear way, with one idea following on from another. This is like the psychiatrist's word association method – 'what comes into your mind when I say . . .?' The Why Why technique (I prefer Why Why Why) illustrates this.

You start with a problem or issue and state it as clearly as you can. That means in words (words are useful when you want to be specific). Then add 'which was caused by' and write down what response comes into your head. Then again, 'which was caused by', and so on.

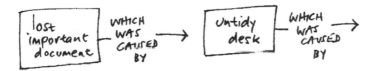

This is another way of working backwards towards a root cause or 'real' problem. It's a great mental keep fit idea. Although this technique seems like a logical analysis of a problem, in fact each link requires creativity. In other words, it might not have occurred to you before, which is why you have a problem. So don't forget to relax and turn on the nice music.

With this or any such technique you are free to choose between boxes or circles (or any shape you can get words into). Choose the one you most associate with creative thinking as that may well help your mind to flow.

Not only can you introduce shapes as you fancy for non-linear thinking, but even apparently linear processes don't have to keep to straight lines. Notice you can abbreviate 'which was caused by' to Why?, Why? – hence the Why Why technique.

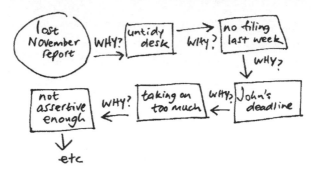

In this case I turned in the opposite direction for the sake of space. You could have gone round the page then spiralled inwards, for instance (or from the middle outwards). If writing the word 'why' more than two or three times becomes a chore you can use the useful symbol -? The arrows between the boxes indicate immediately which *direction* you are thinking in. This is a vital aspect of the way we think (eg from the general to the particular or from the particular to the general) and it is completely accommodated by the little arrow pointers.

'How To' hierarchy

While we are on hierarchy pictures, the so-called How To technique is another winner. This is based on the common sense that you usually don't just need to know what to do, but How To do it. Unless you know *how*, you may not be able to move forward towards your goal, however great your knowledge.

In this case, put How To in front of each goal, aim etc. Thus, not 'get rich', but 'How To get rich'. The clever part is that your answer should always be another How To question.

(Good questions are better than bad answers anyway, and if a
good question takes you three-quarters of the way to a
solution a succession of good questions will do miracles.) You
still need your creativity, so keep relaxing. Let's start simple.
After 'How To get rich', perhaps 'How To make money'.
Then, 'How To get a better paid job'. Then, maybe 'How To
get some qualifications'. Notice that you could have gone off
in any direction after 'How To make money'. Such as: 'How

To choose a business venture' or
'How To win on the horses' and so
on. That's where the tree or
hierarchy picture comes in.
Notice I have abbreviated How
To to HT – anything that
speeds up a technique will
help to capture a flow of
creative ideas.

This overall picture is useful. As with the earlier diagrams,
you can see at a glance all your options. That provides a
delightful, holistic, right-brain perspective on the
situation. For most people this works better than a list, or
several lists, of words. The magic is when you get so far
down branches and twigs that the answers become
blindingly obvious. For instance, if you get to 'HT get on
night school course', the next might be 'HT get a local
college brochure'. Answer: 'get your phone book, pick up
the phone and ask for one'. This is something you can *do*.

Once you get down to a 'to do' list level of task, and you
can't think of any more HTs, provided you keep your
creative juices flowing you have cracked the problem.

That doesn't mean you are rich, super fit, or have a complete solution to a previously intractable problem. Rather, it means you are not *stuck* with your problem. You know what to do next and (importantly) How To do it. That means you can move away from A, where you don't want to be, towards B where you want to be. Things are once again in your control, and you achieved that control yourself. As a bonus, it's a lot more fun doing things using your own rather than other peoples' brainpower.

The other advantage of this blossoming tree is that you have a number of HT options, or routes, to follow. One characteristic of right-brain thinking is that you come up with options and *never* a final answer. The right-brain never goes to bed and might well bubble up with an even better idea out of the blue a few days on. The left-brain tends to accept the first feasible possibility it identifies, and then treats it as *the* solution. But even the left side of your brain is no slacker. However, it will more than likely spend its time on justifying *why it was right* – even in the face of more recent evidence, or patently better ideas in the meantime.

According to your creative brain, any one of your HT routes will potentially get you where you want to be, even though some will inevitably turn out to be nonsense. So you can pursue more than one and increase the odds of success. That's not as impractical as it might seem. The fact is that the further you go down your branches the more certainly HT questions will start to repeat themselves. In effect you are beginning to identify the key HTs (how to *knowledge* and *know-how*) to success. This is equivalent to identifying a root problem, having started with the ostensible, or presented problem. Try it. Use a real problem.

HT . . .

Don't underestimate the life-changing power of the HT technique. En route you will meet thought-provoking destinations such as:

The HT questions will accurately reflect your own situation and needs, of course – something that would take a counsellor months, perhaps. It's your brain's way of sorting things out and offering a creative way forward. Something pops into your conscious mind from your unconscious.

These sorts of questions, however life-changing they seem, are all within your control. It is invaluable information if you are prepared to act on it.

You've no one to blame for your lot in life. Your future is – as far as it can be for human beings – in your own hands.

No problem is too hard for you to face with confidence.

Your creative brain operates round the clock.

Creating opportunities

The opportunity circle is a good technique for generating opportunities. It follows the standard brainstorming formula but introduces association, or relationships, which are an important aspect of lateral thinking. Most eureka type ideas come from linking otherwise disparate things, for instance something in nature with an engineering problem. You start the opportunity circle by thinking of the different issues involved in a problem or a topic you want to explore. For example, if you are exploring opportunities to expand your business you may need to consider:

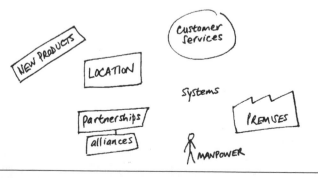

And so on. In this case your quota is 12 issues or topics, which match the numbers on your clock-face opportunity circle.

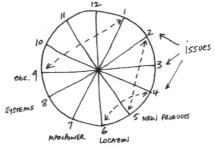

Throw a dice to choose a random number to go with number one and brainstorm these two issues together. For example, you might consider new products in relationship to some outside alliance, merger, acquisition, agency or partnership arrangement. Pursuing this thought train, you need not consider developing in-house products (possible already given attention), and may be able to reach growth goals more quickly. Similarly, by linking customer services with premises, you will need to explore aspects of premises that will facilitate better customer services. What would your customers prefer, for instance? Are your premises designed with you or them in mind? Each combination presents a new angle on the subject, and will usually produce opportunities you may not have thought of without such simple prompting.

This is a fairly high-level business example, but each issue can be subjected to the same process. Systems, for example, become the main subject for brainstorming and the 12 issues surrounding the topic are again related randomly. By throwing a dice it means you will not give weight and time to ideas you have already thought of, or the most obvious ones. You need to be open to any combination of the various issues. If the relationship seems strange and unfruitful, better still, as the best ideas usually arise from the most unlikely combinations. As we saw earlier, an advantage of achieving a quota of issues or ideas means that you will have to stretch your creativity to include issues you would not normally have ever thought of. These, when combined with better-understood topics, are ripe for fruitful opportunities.

Chapter 5

Solving Problems

In this chapter:

◆ **A few well-known problem-solving techniques that incorporate some graphical element.**

Most problem-solving techniques incorporate graphics in one way or another. In this chapter I give some well-known examples. Don't get hung up on the titles of these techniques. I use the best-known descriptions so that you will recognise them if you come across them. But in any case they appear in different formats.

These are *creative* problem-solving techniques, although they usually add some form of analysis, so they tend to combine left- and right-brain thinking operations. The visual ideas techniques you have met so far remain valid, and especially the need for a creative approach. In fact brainstorming-type thinking applies in just about any problem-solving situation. It is the foundation to any creative technique, however sophisticated. You need intuition, insight and the odd eureka. In short, something more than a cold analysis of the problem and the 'facts' could ever provide. Even the popular 'pros and cons' have to be identified in the first place, and will probably differ from one person to the next. If you can solve your problem by following a known process, fine.

But if your problem can be reduced to simple rules and logic, it hardly ranks as a problem. It's when you get stuck that you need ways to employ more creative methods in order to harness your unconscious mind.

However dire your problem, you need to relax and get into a creative mode. That takes practice and a little know-how in relaxation techniques.

The methods you have already met for getting ideas can all be used for solving problems. Problems, more than anything, require good ideas and a fertile imagination. As we saw earlier, whether you define an issue as a problem or an opportunity is not important anyway. With the right mental approach they are two sides of the same coin. It's a matter of choosing the tool that helps you to get whatever you want (whatever you call it) in a way that works best for you.

However, some traditional problem-solving methods add some sort of analysis to the basic idea creation process. Some are particularly useful for defining the problem more accurately, or getting to the root problem. Some add a structure that appeals to more left-brain dominant people, whilst still incorporating creative principles.

The techniques you will meet in this chapter will provide further examples of how graphics, or pictures form an important part of the problem-solving process. Add these to the less structured methods you have already met, and you will be ready to tackle just about any problem, now using your whole brain.

The problem-solving process

You can represent the process of problem solving in a diagrammatic, sequential way. For example:

This is just one example, but many models follow a similar, logical theme. Notice that at each stage you may have to do decide which 'facts' need to be taken into account, what assumptions to make and so on. In other words you need to do some creative thinking, however mundane your problem. Creativity starts with defining the problem. A problem is not always the one that first comes to mind (the 'presented' problem). Any of the methods we met in the previous chapter will help to redefine the problem or issue.

Sometimes it helps to approach a problem using a particular approach or model, and the brain seems to respond to this described spatially. Notice that in this model both the left and right sides of the brain are called into play at each stage in the process. In some text book models the creative element in problem-solving is often overlooked (and the 'frustration factor' is rarely even mentioned). When using words only, the creative brain doesn't seem to be turned on anyway – hence the need for stimulation in more visual, spatial or right-brain mode.

Force field analysis

Force field analysis explores the positive and negative forces within a problem or situation – what is working for you and what is working against you.

It's a simple enough concept, but it can be a useful way to bring together objectively the many factors at work in most problems. In this case simple arrows depict the forces at work and concentrate the mind.

Briefly state the FORs and AGAINSTs along the opposing arrows. You may wish to brainstorm these, using some of the techniques 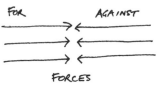 in the previous chapter. Showing these factors in a graphical way reminds you that there are always pluses and minuses – pros and cons. If you don't have such a selection (including negative forces) you don't really have a problem. Life is like that – few things are black and white. You've heard the maxims: 'Every cloud has a silver lining'; 'It's an ill wind . . .' etc. If you can't spot the opposing forces at work, you may have missed something and may well have a bigger problem than you thought.

Of course drawing lines and arrows doesn't identify what the various forces are in your particular problem. That requires creative thinking and is a right-brain function that simply does not lend itself to ABC methods and logical checklists. You've got to use your whole brain. However, as with the simple wheel and spoke type diagrams you have met, a graphical format helps your thinking. It doesn't constrain you to left to right, top to bottom lists or prose.

Depending on whether you are an optimist or a pessimist you will tend to naturally come up with either positive or negative factors or forces. That's fine, as the discipline of this method requires you to think of opposing forces to whatever comes to mind. If you come up with lots of factors in your favour, you need to concentrate on identifying negative factors – things that are likely to scupper your attempts or work against you. If you can only think of obstacles and negative forces, then a bit of forced optimism, or positive thinking, is called for. The idea is to strengthen positive forces, as well as reduce or eliminate negative forces. That demands new ideas and a brainstorming approach. Most of all, you need to understand yourself and get in touch with your unconscious mind where so much of clever problem-solving is done.

Let's say your problem is that you need to get a particular qualification to help you in your job and increase your prospects, but with home and social commitments you just don't seem to have the time.

Start by quickly and instinctively listing positive and negative forces in a force field diagram.

Positive might be:

- ◆ You're still fairly young and will learn quickly if you set your mind to it.
- ◆ Perhaps your employer will give financial assistance or time off work.
- ◆ Maybe you enjoy the subjects you will learn and look forward to study with pleasure.

Against this:

- ◆ You may feel guilty about not spending time with your children.
- ◆ You may have started the course of study in the past and did not complete it for whatever reason, so you are not confident of your sticking power.
- ◆ Maybe your spouse is not behind you in this.
- ◆ Maybe you don't have a suitable place in the house where you can study in peace and quiet. And so on.

Here is the force field picture format, suitably abbreviated to save time, as new issues may pop quickly into your mind.

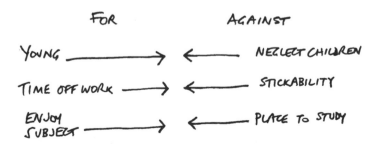

It is almost certain that however positive you are you will easily identify negatives. In many cases you will be able to easily overcome them. It is just a matter of taking account of factors that may potentially affect your problem. Similarly, even a naturally negative person should be able to identify positive forces, even if it is just seeing another angle on the situation. Moreover, negative forces will seem obvious to a negative person, while positive forces will seem just as obvious to a positive thinker. The tendency is thus to omit the obvious. But it is important to include all the forces that come to mind in your diagram anyway. It's a useful checklist and helps your overall thinking process. Sometimes one factor reminds you of several others. A negative suggests a positive and vice versa. Just seeing positive factors in black and white helps your attitude and motivation. At the same time, by getting down all the downsides there is less danger of kidding yourself as to the seriousness of a situation.

You will probably find that each factor has its own level of importance and significance. Some will be minor factors you hardly thought it worth writing down, whilst others might be vital to your success. That is, each has a different weighting or force, as well as direction (positive or negative). You can easily adapt your diagram to these variables, such as by using different thicknesses of force arrows.

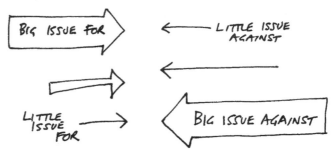

There are no rules for these sorts of techniques. Draw whatever you like if it can be useful. If you are into numbers you can give each factor a numerical weighting. For instance a positive might be a ten and two twos. But on the other side you have two negatives weighted about five each, plus a minor one.

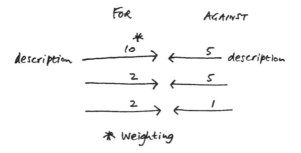

The idea is that at any time the forces are in equilibrium, with the positive and negative forces counteracting each other. You could show this either arithmetically (giving a numerical weighting to each factor) or graphically, with thick and thin, or short and long arrows.

Don't split hairs. Your weightings can be percentages, adding up to a hundred, or each side can add up to ten or 20 if you just have a few factors. Each side doesn't even have to add up to the same figure. But by making it something close, you acknowledge the fact that both positive and negative forces have a part to play, and that some sort of equilibrium exists. The weighting of positive and negative forces respectively should reflect not just the importance of each factor to the overall problem, but the level of time and effort you need to give to them.

The finished diagram will give you an overall impression of how you fare in your problem. The idea is to maximise and enhance any positive factors as far as you can, and to minimise or eliminate any negative factors (which is why you first need to clearly identify them). For instance, a couple of positive factors may have the effect of reducing a big negative force.

You may be surprised at how creative you become when dealing with a real, live problem using force field analysis. The anticipation of a solution that will give you pleasure acts as a strong motivator, both for right-brain creativity and left-brain application, rationale and effort. However, don't kid yourself. Initially, at least, try to overstate the downsides of a situation, leaving yourself with the challenge of bringing positive forces to bear.

As with most graphical problem-solving tools, you can use it in flexible, creative ways. You don't need a problem, for instance. You could use this and similar techniques to consider an *opportunity*, or to help you make an

important decision in your life, such as regarding a job or
career change or a house move.

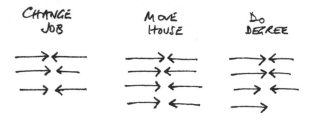

You don't need to define the problem specifically, at least
at this stage. The process of identifying forces will
elucidate your problem and suggest solutions. It might
turn out, for instance, that a single negative factor
constitutes your true problem, and that's the 'force' you
need to tackle. Or maybe you have more than one
problem, of a different nature, requiring a different
approach. Either way, that's useful knowledge. Ignorance
– especially self-ignorance – is the most serious kind of
problem of all. 'Forces' may be internal rather than
external, and involve
your own strengths
and weaknesses,
beliefs and attitudes.

Notice also that 'forces' will differ depending on whether
they are inside or outside your control.

Things you can overcome personally, even tricky, complex matters, don't usually produce the headaches that come from things that are in other people's hands or the lap of the gods. You can take account of this important difference in your creative diagrams, such as by the use of different colours. Or simply adjust the weighting, effectively increasing the impact of a negative factor that you don't have much control over. Lack of control, or *perceived* lack of control (you feel helpless to change things), may be a large part of the problem.

As a third alternative, identify people problems, such as the need to persuade or convince someone, to get authority, or to get someone out of the decision loop, as problems (forces) in their own right. In each of these cases you may well identify positive forces also, such as people who you can use to influence things positively.

'How To' diagram

'How' is an important problem-solving question. You don't just need to know what to do, but how to do it. Otherwise, seemingly 'solved' problems will tend to remain as problems. A 'solution' might be a problem in a different guise. The How To technique simply applies the 'how' question at every stage, rephrases questions in How To format and creatively explores any How To direction imaginable.

Using the same example as in the force field analysis above, a goal of 'To pass so-and-so examination' would become 'How To pass so-and-so examination (be specific, of course).'

As each aspect of the How To goal comes to mind (just like factors in a force field analysis) simply make sure you accommodate the How To prefix. Then automatically each obstacle, mini target, stepping-stone goal or difficulty will be phrased in this practical, focused way.

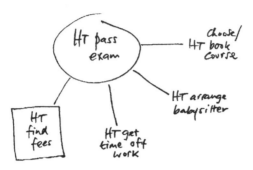

And so on.

The How To diagram then forms a hierarchy as each question leads to another – usually a more immediate, shorter-term step to the goal.

How to find the fees, for instance, might suggest:

And so on.

The hierarchical graphics help with this process, just like a flow-chart. By using this free format you can add extra How Tos along any branches of the tree (or cascade) as they occur to you. The diagram is never fully complete.

That, of course, is a feature of creative as against logical, sequential thinking. You always allow room for a better solution, which your unconscious mind may have tucked away somewhere.

As with most creative techniques, it is best to do this quickly and instinctively. Otherwise you will tend to judge, evaluate and maybe dismiss what might turn out to be valuable insights.

Don't be surprised if you tend to repeat How To questions, even when coming to an aspect of the problem from a different direction (down a different branch). This simply confirms you have an important How To to deal with which may be a key to your success.

You can apply this technique to just about any level of problem. For instance, it works at a higher, more strategic level:

A middle HT problem level:

Or at the lowest, most immediate level just like a 'to do' list:

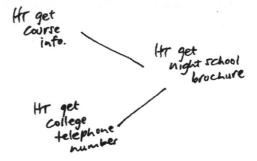

When you arrive at obvious 'to dos', or you start to wonder just what your problem was, you know the technique is working. Something has happened in your mind, which is where problems are solved.

This is a flexible, highly practical technique that just about guarantees you have to address the right questions to solve your initial, presented problem.

Watch out for spin-off benefits from this sort of technique. In this example, for instance, you might learn in the process how to save money on things you don't really need which will have benefits far above your specific training course needs. At the same time don't get depressed if you seem to come up with new problems you hadn't thought about. Problems don't go away just because you don't identify them. And worse, they have a habit of turning out to be much bigger later. Nevertheless, stay positive. Every problem is an opportunity to find a How To solution, and pick up some useful learning in the process.

Note I have abbreviated How To as HT when doing a diagram. This is so as not to slow down the process and lose the intuitiveness and flow of ideas. When it comes to the graphical part, create your own system. I have found that 'top down' cascade or tree type diagrams work well.

You can do this top-down or left-right, whatever you are comfortable with and which seems to generate the most ideas.

Occasionally you will use a 'hub and spoke' layout like a mind map.

This is useful when you are in brainstorming mode and you want to generate as many HTs as possible quickly, without worrying about layout or presentation. You may then wish to produce a more finished product in cascade, or tree and branch style as above.

However, I suggest you stick to the How To terminology – the words How To or an abbreviation. Language affects the way we think in surprising ways, and in this case produces practical rather than theoretical ideas.

Lotus blossom

This technique was developed by Yasuo Matsumura, president of Clover Management, a Japanese company. It uses the idea of a lotus flower, but also incorporates the ideas of the Lotus 123 computer spreadsheet software. This is based on squares, built up as matrices of nine squares. It's a bit squary for lotus blossom petals but the name has stuck.

Write the problem or issue in the central square – this is equivalent to your central theme in a wheel and spoke diagram. Ideas are then written in the surrounding eight squares, equivalent to the brainstormed 'spoke' ideas, or main branches in a hierarchy or cascade sort of picture. Each of the eight ideas is then transferred to the centre of the adjacent, outer lotus petal. This becomes the new topic, idea or redefined problem. You then subject each topic to the same brainstorming process, aiming for a further quota of eight ideas.

You will need a big sheet of paper, but it is useful to see the whole process on one sheet, rather than transferring each main subtopic to separate sheets, as you might with the graphical methods we have met so far. For practical purposes you will have to keep to just a few words in each square, but this is also a handy discipline.

It means you have to boil everything down to simple terms. As long as you know what you mean by a short phrase, or even a single word, the technique will work fine.

This incorporates some principles of creative thinking. One is the hierarchy of ideas method in which topics or issues branch off, with smaller branches in turn for subsidiary topics and issues. This allows you to pursue an idea, in different directions or in greater depth.

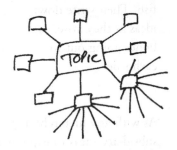

Another principle is that of a quota of ideas. This means you have to keep thinking of ideas until you have reached a certain number, in this case eight.

This is compatible with the idea that the unconscious brain is more or less unlimited and, theoretically, you need never stop getting ideas, even on apparently the most mundane of subjects. Rationally, you would probably stop at the first 'great' idea you thought of, which presupposes – quite wrongly – that it is also the best. Eight is a compromise but you needn't lose sleep if you cannot come up with a quota of ideas. Eight happens to fit the nine-square pattern of the lotus technique nicely.

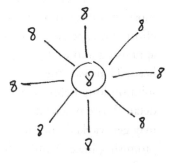

Fishbone diagram

A fishbone diagram helps to get new ideas and solve difficult problems. Write the problem at the head of the fish. Then write down ideas as they arise, as bones going out to each side.

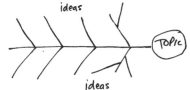

As with any hierarchy type diagram you can add further subsidiary ideas to expand a topic or line of enquiry. As with any brainstorming process, you can generate as many ideas as you like. Simply add on extra bones to the diagram. You may wish to rearrange your diagram after the initial draft, to make plenty of space for ideas requiring lots of subsidiary bones. Arrange your ideas from the simplest or most promising at the head to the most complicated, or those requiring the most time, effort and expense, at the tail end. Similarly, when appraising and evaluating ideas to implement, start at the head. That way, the chances are that you will arrive at a solution long before you need to consider all the ideas in detail. More practically, if you start at the tail end you may get waylaid and never get round to the most promising ideas. Unlike the lotus blossom diagram with its fixed number of cells, you can have as long or short a fishbone as you like, and as unnatural a bone structure as you like to allow for extra ideas as they occur.

Chapter 6

Giving a Speech or Presentation

In this chapter:

◆ **You'll never be lost for words if you don't**
   depend **on them. Use more of your natural**
   visual and graphical abilities to do a better
   overall job of communication.

Speeches and public presentations have accounted for more
sleepless nights than even the most frightening human feats.
It is said to be the number one phobia among managers and
professional people. Which of course is all very irrational.
But that doesn't help much if you can't help how you feel.

The textbooks will give you all the standard advice.

All this is sound advice. Dry marker pens and out-of-
focus projectors are almost a standard feature of amateur
presentations. Blown bulbs seem to be too much for

modern technology – or rather mediocre presenters – to cope with. That's nothing to do with stage fright and such hang-ups. It's simply commonsense to get such things right and disrespectful of any audience if you don't. For instance, if possible, get familiar with the venue before you turn up. At worst, check on the condition of any equipment and what to do of it dies on you. Be as independent as possible anyway, for instance by bringing your own supply of marker pens.

Horses for presentational courses

Before thinking about pictures, I will first address the question of whether you read out a speech, give it from notes or extemporise. Different considerations apply, so it's horses for courses.

In the case of an impromptu speech, such as when you are jumped on to 'say a few words' you have little choice other than to decline, which you often later regret and which, as a habit, can sometimes be career limiting. But paradoxically these are the least problematical cases, as you don't have long enough to worry and torment yourself, and it usually involves a very short speech which is soon over.

Usually there are precedents and tradition about speeches and presentations to fall back on, especially in a work or professional context. For instance, many formal speeches, say to an institute or society, are read out word for word. The advantage of this for the presenter is that you can prepare carefully and make every word count. It also makes it easier to judge timing, which is why conference organisers prefer it.

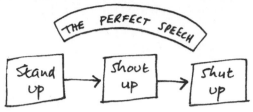

The advantage for the audience is that they are spared flannel, personal off-the-cuff insertions, and the usual amateurs' unending conclusions. Best of all, verbatim speeches are usually over a lot more quickly.

Presentations with notes – to whatever degree – are by far the biggest cause for concern and will apply in the majority of situations. Precedent also applies here. Most wedding speeches, for example, are well prepared with notes but not often read out verbatim.

If you can conquer presentations of different sorts using brief notes you will soon develop the confidence to speak off the cuff now and again. You will usually have a few minutes' preparation time anyway. If you are not given any time to prepare, your audience will make allowances anyway (provided you discreetly let them know it). That is, you get a sympathy vote. The big problem area – that you can do much about – is when working from notes, which is what we will consider here.

There is a big difference between a five-minute stand-up address, a two-hour workshop and a one-day seminar, of course. Fortunately most of the principles of good communication apply generally. Foremost is the fact that the visual sense is the most important and you will not get far without exploiting it in your presentation.

Making a visual impact

That doesn't mean you need high-tech gadgets or professionally prepared slides or transparencies. 'Visual' is not confined to visual aids. You are the biggest visual element in the presentation and (potentially) the most compelling picture. It's part of the deal that  people watch you, at least until you give them enough reason to turn away their eyes as well as stop their ears. People see a lot. They will see you putting your hands in your pockets, for instance, or repeatedly scratching, when you have no knowledge of your behaviour whatsoever. They can spot the most innocuous mannerisms and minor bodily aberrations, especially if you cannot occupy their minds with the content of your presentation.

We are more stimulated by movement, so a moving visual object gets more attention and adds potentially to the effectiveness of a group or large audience presentation.

This doesn't mean flailing your arms around, as that sort of movement can be tiring, embarrassing and annoying to your audience. Plus, it is a rule that you should act *congruently*. In other words, what you say and how you say it should honestly match.

Another rule is to be yourself. This being the case, a person who naturally uses a lot of body movement will do more damage trying to avoid it than pretending they are more controlled. Conversely, a person who contrives to make inappropriate gestures or become uncharacteristically intense will be quickly exposed. Moreover, you don't have to know a person well to do that sort of shrink-like appraisal. From childhood we develop the skill of spotting incongruence in the way people communicate. Audiences often make allowances for nerves, inexperience and even incompetence (we're all human) but they don't like fakes.

Some professionals incorporate the visual movement requirement by walking away from the lectern a few paces and returning every so often throughout the speech. This is just the optical break people need to keep their attention.

You fulfil the same function when moving to and from an OHP or flip chart. I usually use two, well separated flip charts, which allows inbuilt mobility between them.

The trick is to keep the attention of the audience, and this is a sensory process – seeing, hearing and feeling. Rather like the cross-eyed discus thrower – he never won any medals but he sure kept the crowd's attention!

Visual aids

An aid should aid. If it doesn't measurably help you to get your message across then do without it. That is a good principle for OHP transparencies, slides and flip charts, and especially for electronic and computer-linked devices. You and your subject are central and not some inanimate gizmo. A human being is potentially the most compelling visual subject, and your visual aids are just to help you.

Applying this principle to visual aids such as a flip chart or OHP usually means keeping to as few words as you can and adding pictures wherever possible (which is nearly always). How many times have you been confronted with a great list of columns and words on a big screen? Or a packed flip chart presumably designed to save paper? The simple neurological fact is there is no possibility of your spectators remembering masses of information, however visually attractive. Even if they manage to take it all in, they probably can't see the wood for the trees, and will miss the important

points. Ordinary humans can't cope with more than half
a dozen bits of information at once. And even *seeing*
much more than that on a single page can be
intimidating when there is no chance of digesting it.

Accountants and other professional people often get this
wrong. Maybe it's because they are already familiar with
the data, or are at home with numbers. The really dumb
ones think that such detail will impress their audience.
Invisible or incomprehensible detail is hard on ordinary
folk who weren't that keen on sitting through the session
anyway. Even if you manage to keep an audience's
attention (which is sometimes a courteous facade anyway),
standard issue brains can only take in a certain amount of
detail anyway, so you will waste everybody's time.

What's on the OHP or flip chart can be as much for your
use as the audience's. Unless you leave the room and let
them peruse your pretty visual aids, you have to say
something for yourself, and that's what communication is
all about. However, you may need a little memory jogger
and a word or two or picture on a prepared visual meets
that need well. Carefully choosing words or a graphical
representation of your subject focuses your mind for a
good communication. The chances are that what makes
sense to you and is easy to remember will fulfil the same
vital role for your audience. So everybody is happy – or
at least well informed – through a simple
communication. More importantly you fulfil the *purpose*
of your communication if you can make it effective – get
your message across to other minds.

Here are the sorts of simple format that will probably do the trick.

Three main points are usually ideal. That's a longstanding speechmaker's rule. More than four is stretching it, as we can only take in about half a dozen chunks of information at one time. However, it is usually a simple matter to break information down. You cannot be too simple when communicating to a group of varying intellect, temperament and sensory preference (as all groups are).

Similarly, keep to one, two or perhaps three words per main point or topic. Choosing these words with care is a sound discipline for any communicator. Better still, they are meaning and memory props for your audience, far easier to absorb and remember than even the shortest 'proper' sentence. Comprehension and memory are multiplied when words are linked to pictures or a spatial format that appeals to the right-side of the brain.

If you need to get a lot on a flip chart or single OHP – such as an organisation chart – you can achieve that better by a 'picture' with, say, peoples' or departmental initials. That gives the overall 'picture'. Detail (if needed, and which is often overdone) can be given as separate sheets in smaller chunks of the chart, reverting back to the summary chart as necessary to maintain the 'overall picture'. More sheets with fewer words usually mean far higher audience attention and comprehension – hence the three point public speaker's wisdom.

A 'picture' in this communication context usually means a diagram of some sort, comprising the simple lines and shapes you have met. It doesn't demand matchstick men or dogs that look like cows, let alone da Vinci stuff. A visual aid 'picture' is simply what your brain can easily classify and compare to create meaning and sense.

Providing an anchor

Use different colours of course – the universal visual aid. The human eye can handle a few million so you will not overtax your spectators' cerebral powers. If you use a different colour for your three key points you can stick to the same colour for each subsequent OHP or flip chart on that theme. That provides what is called an anchor, which helps the audience to register the information in mental pigeonholes.

A recurring little picture or symbol will also act as an anchor. Similarly, you can make good use of two flip charts. For instance, use one for pros and the other for cons, one for strengths and the other for weaknesses and so on. If the training budget doesn't run to two flip charts, a dividing line down the middle does a similar job, except that your movement between the two helps to keep the audience visually alert. Again, use a different colour for each column. And if you choose green as good and red as bad, keep to those colours as an anchor. Thus, even when wielding the appropriately coloured marker as you speak, you reinforce your message in your spectators' unconscious minds.

You don't have to be an artist to produce very effective visual aids. Just keep to these principles and keep your pictures as simple as possible. A perfectly straight line, or truly circular circle, can be very boring. A few imperfections will give your imperfect audience something interesting to look at.

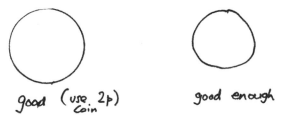

good (use 2p)   good enough
    coin

If you use simple pictures you need not prepare them in advance as OHP transparencies or flip charts. You will add to the visual movement and maintain attention much better by drawing *as you speak*. A couple of practice sessions will soon have you confident. If you wish you can pre-do the words, which will remind you of what to draw. Alternatively you can pre-do the pictures, which will remind you of the words. That way you have spelling to contend with, of course. Also, people seem more interested in watching someone draw shapes and pictures than words, which we got enough of at school. An incomplete visual – with words or pictures missing – can be more compelling than a complete one. The mind looks for meaning, and if it can't get it immediately it will be curious, momentarily at least, to find it and mentally put to bed any communication. But don't overdo it as 'meaning' might be that you are incompetent or incoherent and your OHPs confirm it.

Graphical aids

You have lots of choice when it comes to graphical aids. As we have seen, squares, circles, triangles and other simple geometric shapes have a myriad of uses. When combined you can illustrate just about anything. The number of points you have may suggest the shape to use. For instance a triangle for three points and a square – perhaps divided into quadrants – for four.

Quadrants can be used in lots of situations. Some of the most well known business models, such as the Boston Matrix or the 4 Ps marketing mix, use quadrants.

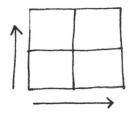

As we saw earlier, usually two sides of the main square will represent dimensions, or scales. In this way your picture tells a lot.

Three circles, clouds or rectangles can just as well represent three points. Draw what takes your fancy, or what seems to fit best with what you want to communicate. Remember you can readily show relationships by overlapping shapes or connecting lines, with or without arrows to denote direction.

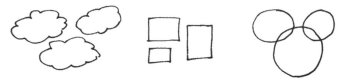

A five-point star is good for five points and is simple to draw when you get the hang of it. I've shown how you do this. Just remember each straight line is the same length and the angle 30 degrees – an averages witch's hat or wigwam. With practice you will do this with panache in a live presentation and get more respect – whatever the imperfections.

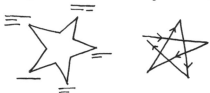

If you need to go to six points you can draw a six-sided star by superimposing an equilateral triangle on to another one, but turning it round. This works even better when you are linking two groups of three. It's also easier to remember, just like a telephone number broken down into smaller chunks.

Ideally you should not go beyond six headings or subheadings, so you don't need complex shapes to help you. For instance, you can usually subdivide a dozen points logically into three fours or four threes.

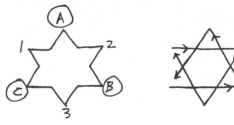

Sometimes the material gives you no choice, such as the case of a diagram with eight or nine 'points'. Even this can be quite digestible with a simple, graphical layout and by using single words. It depends on the communication 'package'. That includes the 'how' as well as the 'what' – the medium (and how you use it) as well as the message.

Keeping to just a few items is not so much because our brain cannot cope with more (on a piece of paper or a chart). After all, the brainstorming type diagrams we used earlier sometimes ran to many branches. It's the fact that a group comprises different levels, preferences and interests. In other words, you have to go for the common denominator, and simplicity is the only reliable formula.

Graphs and graphics

Common pictures for presentations include graphs, and their equivalent in bar charts, pie charts and such like. Again, you will just apply common geometrical shapes to help communicate what you need to. Most people prefer comparisons of say years, products or divisions in pictures than in numbers or words. Usually you don't need great accuracy in any case to make a point. Most people prefer shapes than the straight lines that ordinary graphs comprise.

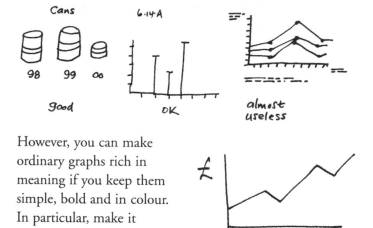

However, you can make
ordinary graphs rich in
meaning if you keep them
simple, bold and in colour.
In particular, make it
absolutely clear what each
axis represents. This is where symbols like £ or $ signs are
worth their weight in marker pens.

New dimensions

3-D is better than 2-D when it comes to graphical
representations and it may be worth trying your skills.
You will be familiar with, for instance, the sort of graphs
that depict soft drink cans or other packages shown in
different sizes to show quantity consumed, beef sales
depicted as cows, property as little houses or factories and
so on. Computer programs take all the sweat out of 3-D
but you need to keep your presentation interpersonal and
not too clinical, detailed or over 'correct'. 3-D per se
doesn't impress anyway, as people are used to high
standards of printed data in the media. It is simply a
more efficient visual communication device, as that's the
way we see things in real life. The absence of 3-D from
the world's flipcharts and hand-drawn OHPs is more to

do with peoples' hang-ups about their drawing skills than effective communication theory.

The aim is simple: to make the strongest possible visual impact, but to keep what you say and the pictures you use appropriate and congruent.

Anything for a laugh

Cartoons have lots of uses. They can get a point across strongly, and are especially useful if the subject is controversial (say between two departments, sections or functions). Humour helps universally in presentations and speeches. Cartoons are also a useful break between main subjects or mini sessions. Because they are visual they keep attention and if they introduce the right level of humour they can also help to set the tone in a meeting or training programme. Professionals also use them for breathing space. A cartoon doesn't need the presenter's explanation, or any comment, so you are free to sort out your notes and prepare for the next topic, unnoticed by your audience whose minds are temporarily occupied. However, cartoons are a specialised area, and apart from borrowing one or two professionally drawn cartoons to add value to a presentation, you will gain more than enough mileage from the simple line drawings you have met. You can apply humour throughout a presentation, through your visual aids, the words you use and body language you adopt. Worse than your average person who thinks he or she can't draw but can (to the level good communication requires) is the person who thinks he or she is an undiscovered cartoonist.

Larger than life

Any words you display, as well as being as few as possible
(in any single transparency or chart) should be visible
from the extreme rear of the room. This applies also to the
captions on cartoons, which may be almost illegible if you
have copied the cartoon from a magazine or newspaper.
These sorts of rules are no more than common courtesy,
and only rank amateurs seem to break them heedlessly. If
you are going to exploit picture power you need to design
and deliver your communication accordingly.

Helping yourself

Visual aids that help the audience to understand your
message will help you to achieve the purpose of your
communication, whether to inform, persuade, motivate,
impress, warn or whatever. That's the test of any
communication, of course. However, visual aids include
more direct self-aid. Probably your presentation notes will
extend beyond using transparencies and flip charts as
reminder cribs, and you will have one or more A4 sheets
of notes close by. In this case, very similar principles
apply. You want your notes to communicate to you what
you mean to talk about, as
effectively as you want your
visual aids to communicate to
your audience. Unlike a
conference or large meeting
presentation, a smallish group
will not put up with much word-
for-word prepared material – if

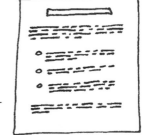

any. It reduces eye contact, sets a formal tone, says little about the presenter's abilities and hardly helps interaction. One method is to summarise headings, subheadings and points in words with bullets and brief narrative.

That is usually fine if words per bullet are few, large enough to be read at a glance and you can easily remember the last point you made. The problem with words is that when you get into a flap they can strangely merge into each other and all you see is a sea of more or less nothing. This is where little pictures help, accompanied perhaps by one or two words in capitals (capitals are terrible to read in sentences and paragraphs but fine for a few words, such as a heading). Not only will a little picture remind you of the subject for which you specifically chose that picture, but also your brain can absorb it so quickly that if need be you can scan three or four of them in an instant and thus check where you are up to. Reading even short phrases from notes takes much longer for most people.

- How much will it cost?
- What is the best venue?
- What will be the starting and finishing times?
- Who will the delegates be?

These notes might translate to:

Multi-sensory messages

Non-visually-dominant people will not be affected by these graphical techniques as much as visually dominant people. But even non-visually-dominant people use their vision – a large part of every human brain is wired up to that end – it's just that they have a preference for another main sense or modality. Thus, in every case, a visual image is a helpful *addition* to the communication (for all sighted people). Moreover, spoken words will appeal to auditory people anyway, so they are typically well provided for in most conventional communication settings such as a training course or sales presentation. In a group, you will certainly find yourself addressing people of different sensory preference, so you cannot afford to skimp on the visual content. As we have seen, it is by far the most important communication sense. And as the visual sense is especially amenable to spatial visual representations – such as the line drawings we have explored in the book – it makes sense to exploit this fact if you want to make your communication effective. In a group situation you will rarely go wrong if you major on visual impact using whatever graphical tools and techniques you can command.

While on this sensory note, you will appeal to touchy feely folk by bringing along to your presentation objects that can be handled – preferably passed round – or that you handle as part of your presentation. Even a book, product or glossy report folder will do the job. Here again this doubles as a strong, moving, visual image. Here is, therefore, a sound presentations rule:

Employ tangible, three-dimensional, textured 'things' to get your message across.

The olfactory factor

Some glossy leaflets and many products also have a distinctive smell. You will soon recognise the kinaesthetic types in an audience, as they will be reluctant to pass on the feelable object (you probably noticed they were touchy-feely over coffee anyway). Smells can do amazing things for the memory and will anchor a point made in, say, a training course for many years to come. How often does a smell or taste take you right back to childhood, for instance?

Whilst 'olfactory methodology' (smells) is not practicable for everyday communication (even when professionally planned and presented), smells compete with the most vivid visual image in the punch they pack when you can legitimately use them. Having said that, you can get deep into any human cortex by a skilful use of simple pictures, supported with interesting sounds (including a nice voice) and feelings. Smells and tastes are a communication bonus. But the senses are linked anyway, and those mouth-watering pictures in fast food outlets and glossy magazines are examples of indirect picture power, and illustrate how the visual sense can ignite other senses to influence buying.

The effect of personal sensory preference applies in any face-to-face presentation, whether in a group or one-to-one where you can hone your methods to take sensory preference into account. So if your customer, coachee or colleague is visually dominant (i.e. when compared with other people, rather than just with his or her other senses) you can major on the visual sense. The chances are that if you know a work colleague well you will already have learnt his or her dominant sense, so you can play to that. Alternatively, you can concentrate on getting your spoken words (sounds – and any other interesting sounds you can bring to the party like using a squeaky marker pen or tapping a pencil) across to an auditorily dominant person, and so on.

Multi-sensory marketing

In a cursory or impromptu meeting, say with a prospective customer, your safest bet is the shotgun or multi-sensory approach, which is the essence of what this chapter describes. Incorporate all three main senses – visual, auditory and kinaesthetic – weighting them in that order. If you fancy acquiring the simple skills to recognise sensory preference quickly, two or three of my other books (including *NLP in 21 Days*) cover this in some detail.

Whether you are addressing one person or a thousand, each person will only absorb so much. As we saw earlier, that's not more than half a dozen 'bits' of information at one time (like digits in a telephone number or points in an argument). Moreover, whatever the numbers or venue, you are communicating with individual people anyway, not an amorphous mass. The principles in this chapter apply universally. Successful human communication is about one mind communicating to one or more other minds in predominantly visual terms.

You can significantly reduce the trauma of a public speech or other presentation, and significantly increase its effectiveness, by applying these visual principles and simple graphical techniques. It's not the usual shrink's phobia cure, but it's positive and it works. Best of all, it's DIY, so you are spared 'experts'.

Chapter 7

Remembering Things

In this chapter:

◆ **How you can make the most of your memory by understanding the role of graphical ideas and techniques.**

Memory uses all five senses, especially vision. If you think back to a friend or teacher at school you may say something like 'I can see her now'. Our language, as is often the case, accurately reflects what is happening in the brain as we 'see' past events with our internal senses. We call this remembering. When 'seeing' a future situation we might call it imagination, daydreaming, visualisation or whatever.

It figures that pictures play a big part in memory, and indeed we know this from research carried out over many years. For instance, most people can remember peoples' faces better than their names. This is a special kind of visual skill that seems to be hardwired into our brain. For example, we can pick out someone we know in a crowd from the scantiest of visual clues. So if you have to remember things – say for an examination or when learning new tasks at work – you can make the job quicker and easier by deliberately employing visual techniques wherever you can. You can enhance your memory power generally using graphical techniques, using the sorts of shapes and pictures you have met through the book.

Memory systems

Most popular memory systems have a strong visual
element. This usually involves symbols, such as numbers
or letters, but images or pictures play a special part.
Pictures in this sense include well-established visual
memories that are part of your life experience. You can
associate these with new sensory inputs (including things
you want to remember) to help you to remember them
better. Pictures on paper, rather than just in the mind,
play a far smaller but still significant part in popular
memory systems. However, as we have seen, they can be
applied to note-taking, giving a presentation etc, the
purpose of which, in each case, is to aid memory.

As used in memory systems, a letter, number or any
symbol is just a shape. In some cases such as O, T, U and
X, letters are very common shapes that we come across
every day in such things as road signs. Although they
figure in words and language, these are just simple shapes
or graphics. Until letters become a word, they don't have
the disadvantages of words and language over simple
pictures when it comes to remembering.

For instance what comes into your mind (other than the
first letter of a word such as a person's name) when you

see the following symbols? That is, if these were not alphabetical letters, what might each bring to mind?

CHIJLOSVX

The mind pictures that these symbols conjure in your mind are useful in various memory techniques. So-called 'peg' systems are a case in point. Numbers, for instance, can be associated with picturable 'things'. For example:

◆ One – bun   ◆ Six – sticks
◆ Two – shoe   ◆ Seven – heaven
◆ Three – tree   ◆ Eight – gate
◆ Four – door   ◆ Nine – wine
◆ Five – hive   ◆ Ten –hen.

These use rhyme as the association, and it is unlikely that you or I would choose all the same associations, even when aiming for a rhyme. In fact any 'picturable association' can be used to help memory. As a rule the first that comes to your mind is usually the best. Put another way, the first thing you 'remember' is easiest to remember. In a technical, brain sense, it means making best use of existing, dense networks of synaptic, electro-chemical connections and the lifetime of multi-sensory images they contain.

Numbers are harder than words, or even letters, to remember for many people. However, if you associate the number 1 with a bun, 6 with sticks etc, you can link numbers, or the numerical order of events (first, second, third), with things that are far easier than numbers to remember – things you can see or picture in your mind.

Let's say you need to remember a list of ten things. This is like remembering prizes in a game show (cuddly toy . . .) or remembering the shopping without a list.

Choose your own random list to test the system. Here are ten things that came to my mind at random:

1. moth
2. tree
3. potato
4. mountain
5. pullover

6. Cadillac
7. wallpaper
8. coffee
9. cardboard box
10. dictionary.

How would you remember this list by using the above bun, shoe, etc peg system?

First, everything in your list is picturable, because it is a thing. (For the moment you don't have to remember nominal, abstract things like discretion, favour, or desire – words or names that you can't see, feel or hear, or put in a wheelbarrow.)

 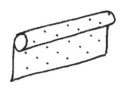 

Second, your peg list is also picturable: you can visualise a bun, a shoe, a gate and so on. All that remains is to put two little pictures together so that you associate each with the other. In this example you would associate a bun with a moth (item number 1), sticks with a Cadillac (item number 6) and so on.

Go down the list of things to remember and associate them in some way with the peg word. For instance you might see a bun filled with moths, a moth delivering buns to the baker, a moth eating cream buns and so on. The secret is to make the visual association, or imagery, as vivid, bizarre or unusual as possible. In other words, as memorable as possible. Once you've thought of a bun full of moths it is hard not to associate a moth with a bun or a bun with a moth. That means you cannot help but remember – which is the way it should be. Memory is something we do expertly all the time with never a conscious thought. It's only in specific, 'conscious' memory situations, such as revising for an exam, preparing for a speech or remembering the names of a group of people that we need to adopt the sort of visual systems that we use unconsciously so well.

It is important to really see your image internally. It is hard to think of an association in a conceptual or abstract way and implant it in your visual cortex. So it will be hard to remember. A visual image needs to be strong if you are to remember it.

Fortunately you can make an image strong and memorable by noticing its colour, size, movement, clarity or fuzziness and any visible details. If any of these characteristics don't grab you, you can intensify them, by exaggerating the colour, size, movement and so on. For example, you will probably remember a half-ton mouse with a green tartan waistcoat better than a standard little grey-brown rodent. Details also help. For example you can notice little antennae on your mental moth and sesame seed on the bun in your brain, and so on.

In practice most people can visualise strong, graphic images in a couple of seconds, and this innate skill lends itself to high-speed memory work.

Proceed down the list and make an association in each case. As with other techniques you have already met for getting creative ideas, the first idea that comes into your mind has special value, however silly or inappropriate it may seem.

FIRST ASSOCIATION

It is your first association. It is literally the first thing that comes to your mind. It follows that your mind will easily make the same association in the future when you need it without doing anything more. The association was, in a sense, already there.

You do it quicker.

FAST

It's faster than waiting for a second or third choice. Having said that, once you have the basic association, or mental link, you can embellish using memory principles, such as making it more bizarre and memorable. That makes it even easier and quicker to remember. Thus, if you instinctively imagine a Cadillac with sticks (item number 6) rather than wheels, you can make the sticks six feet long, see the car walking on its sticks and so on.

The *association*, rather than the things themselves, makes the memory link. The *unforgettable element* makes it unforgettable. You can make a mind picture as bizarre as you like.

So far so easy. How then do you remember the random list of ten items? First, you can easily memorise your peg list in minutes. The fact that there is rhyme makes it even easier, but your visual powers are more than enough to remember the list for life. For instance, you might simply associate two with two shoes and three with three trees. Then your door might have a house number 4 on it, your hive could be pentagonal – five sided – and so on. With a few minutes' time and effort you will memorise the list, which you can then use repeatedly, for life, for any memory feat. In no time it becomes *impossible* not to associate a number with its peg image. Try it. Make whatever association you like and try to forget it by tomorrow.

You can immediately check out your memory power. Just go down your peg list. As soon as you think of bun (1), you will think of a moth. The instant you think of a shoe (2), you will think of a tree, and so on. Pictures are powerful memory aids whether in your mind or, as we have already seen, when transferred to paper.

Remembering numbers

You can also use a peg system to remember numbers. Let's say you want to remember your new cash card Pin which is 3688. The equivalent peg pictures are:

◆ tree (3) ◆ sticks (6) ◆ gate (8) ◆ gate (8)

Check back to the peg list earlier if you need to remind yourself where these words have come from. To establish a memory all you need to do now is link these together in a sort of story or chain of events. For instance, a tree chopped into sticks to make two gates. To make the initial connection when you need to draw cash, your tree can be a cash tree sprouting ten pound notes.

Stories are even easier than individual images to remember as they take on special meaning. We each experience sequences of events or 'stories' each minute and hour of our lives so we get good at it.

The secret is meaning. Something that has meaning *to you* is easy to remember. The meaning, however, does not have to be logical or rational. Rather, it has to be *picturable* or imaginable or, more specifically, amenable to sensory – all five senses – representation.

The idea of meaning or sense is fundamental. Even the most bizarre dreams have meaning, or significance, in the context of our unconscious mind where they take place. The physiological changes that accompany them, like sweating and calling out, as well as REMs (rapid eye movements) confirm that that part of our mind doesn't treat them lightly. So the most stupid story lines are fine for memory purposes. Indeed, were it not for the fact that dreams happen outside of waking consciousness our conscious minds might be overwhelmed by thousands of literally unforgettable experiences. You can only recall those that slip into your conscious mind (on wakening – and perhaps just for fleeting moments). You in effect *reregister* them in your conscious mind. The bottom line on remembering is:

This applies to remembering anything, including numbers. I have illustrated this technique with a four-digit number. In fact you can memorise a number of any length just as easily. Simply create a longer story line. An individual digit can repeat itself in a longer number. You simply give the standard number association a different role in the storyline. That's easy. You can imagine a tree or a gate, for instance, in a hundred situations, any one of which could form part of your memory story line.

Even the most sceptical 'memory like a sieve' people are amazed at their ability to use mind pictures in this way. And you get both quicker and more efficient with practice.

Other memory techniques

The bun-shoe-peg system is just one example. Other systems apply different objects/things to each number. If you wish you can create your own. The associations do not need to rhyme. The chances are that there are things you already associate with each of the numbers from your own lifetime experience so, provided you can count from one to ten, you have nothing, or precious little, new to actually remember.

You can use pictures in other important ways to help your memory. We have already seen how useful shapes such as a wheel and spokes, or a tree-type hierarchy can be. These apply in note-taking, preparing a training session or other presentation, revising for exams – any situation where you need to use your memory to the full. You can also incorporate shapes, icons and simple pictures within these spatial formats to make remembering even easier. The trick is to choose little pictures that *already* have strong associations for you personally. In other words, you have nothing to remember.

As we saw, you can also label files – or anything – with simple pictures or icons. They are used extensively in computer software, and can speed up recognition in the same way as a company logo.

Some memory experts visualise a familiar room or building and use the various objects in them as memory pegs on which to hang whatever they want to remember. Once you have associated each item you want to remember with a familiar object (a settee, picture, fireplace, table, cat basket or whatever) in a familiar position, you just need to do a mental circumnavigation (clockwise or anticlockwise) to trigger the association and hence the items to remember. The same rules of silliness and humour apply to associations. Each location becomes the bun, shoe or tree of the earlier peg system.

Organising to remember

Your brain organises or pigeon-holes information into subjects or categories so that you can quickly allocate any new sensory input to a familiar slot. Things have meaning to you once you incorporate them into your personal, mental filing system.

By forming otherwise unmemorable words into a simple shape that has meaning – such as a tree with branches – you can immediately make them easier to remember.

Here are two sets of words. Which would you find it easier to remember?

Set 1

Pine elm pansy garden wild banyan plants
delphinium conifers dandelion redwood palm ash
violet daisy tropical chestnut flower spruce lupin
buttercup trees deciduous mango willow rose

Set 2

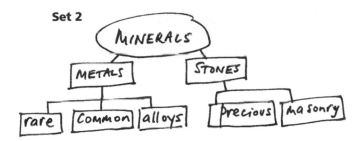

Most people would choose the second set. You might not remember them all but you would probably score quite well. That's because the words form a structure or shape that reflects a special meaning. Most importantly a simple pattern, such as a hierarchy or tree shape, can be pictured more easily.

The first set of words can form an equivalent hierarchy of meaning (have a go), but until you can picture them in that way they will be hard to remember without a special technique such as the peg system you have just met.

Pictures add a dimension of meaning that words alone cannot achieve in communication. We saw this earlier in the way a well-designed flip chart or OHP can communicate even complex concepts when pages of words would only confuse. The same advantages apply to remembering. In fact the power of pictures is a feature of the way we think. A gripping novel can communicate effectively and at the same time is memorable. But in this case you remember the inner pictures and feelings you create as you experience the story yourself, rather than a hundred thousand words comprising hundreds of thousands of character-symbols that have no meaning other than as words and symbols.

Unfortunately we don't get as excited about most of the sorts of information we need to remember, as we do by a gripping novel. That's when pictures help in bridging the gap between none-too-exciting words and your brain's memory system, based as it is on sensory – especially visual – representations. When it comes to flying, we learn from birds. When it comes to swimming or sailing, we learn from fish. When it comes to remembering, we learn from what little we know about human memory, mind-pictures and all.

As you become more confident at drawing and using pictures you will realise new ways in which you can communicate better, enhance your memory and be more productive and fulfilled as a person.